monyul

Land of Monpas

J.S.P. Singh

BlueRose ONE.com
Stories Matter
New Delhi • London

BLUEROSE PUBLISHERS
India | U.K.

BlueRose ONE.com
Stories Matter
NewDelhi • London

For permissions requests or inquiries regarding this publication, please contact:

BLUEROSE PUBLISHERS
www.BlueRoseONE.com
info@bluerosepublishers.com
+91 8882 898 898
+4407342408967

ISBN: 978-93-5704-194-2

Cover design: Shivam
Typesetting: Namrata Saini

First Edition: January 2024

Foreword

Tsering Gyurme
Minister Industries, Textile & Handicrafts
Government of Arunachal Pradesh
Tel : 91 - 360 - 212 948(O)
212 625(R)
Fax : 214 290(R)

FOREWORD

It is a great pleasure to understand that a book depicting the religion, faith, social custom, art and culture of the people of west Kameng District is being published.

Shri J S P Singh has been intimately associated with this area sharing personal experiences and closeness with the people here. His personal endeavor to acquaint with the religion, customs and upliftment of this place also deserves credit. I congratulate his efforts to bring out the rich experience shared by him in our area in respect to the social life. It is my personal privilege to have known him during his tenure in this region.

I am also thankful to him for accepting my suggestion to name the book MONYUL - The land of Monpas

I am confident that this book will benefit and add to the knowledge of all including the people of MONYUL.

(Tsering Gyurme)

Introduction

This book is not a research work. I had the opportunities to remain in close contact with the people of Kameng frontier Division of NEFA from Nov' 65 to Oct' 72 and again from May 1981 to January 1988. During these years I got opportunities to tour Kameng, Subansiri, Siyang, Lohit and Tirap all the five frontier divisions. The little knowledge about the mythology, history, religion, beliefs, social customs, handicrafts and way of living of the people of Kameng were gained only after many years of close interaction with them.

I was first irresistibly attracted to Buddhism practiced in the area, by the picturesque Gompa, the wall paintings inside them, the Kakaling built at the entrance of each village, the stone Mane alongside the tracks, the engraved images on the stones kept in the Mane and the mystic writings on them OM MANE PEME HUM. During that long stay at Dirang, Tawang, Jhang, Lumla and Zimithang I extensively toured the area. I was fortunate to have company of my collegue Shri Pema Wangchuk. Area organizer S.S.B. who introduced me to the tenants, beliefs and practices of Buddhism.

All these experiences and little knowledge could not have been produced by me, if I was not encouraged by my mentor and guide Shri Jank kumar, I.P.S. He created the confidence in me to write this book. I have no words to express my gratitude for him.

Besides the many villagers, I am most grateful to Kesang of Vill- Muchut, Pangchen area, the blind old man Meme

Seng Gombu of Vill- Shakti, Lamas of Tawang Monastery, the progressive young man of Vill- Dirang, Tsering Gyurme, Group Leaders of S.S.B. Nam Tshring and Rinching Dorjee. Rinchin Khandu of Vill - Lish, Sange Monpa of Vill – Namshu, Rinching Phunsto the Painter, Lama Rapten of Rama Camp, Rinchin Dorjee, Pema Dorjee and Khandu Sinjoni of Rupa and my Aka and Miji friends who contributed valuably to my knowledge.

During my tours Shri Chhanglu of village – SERU accompanied me every where and interpreted the book "Karchhak" kept in every Gompa. He deserves my sincere thanks.

My wife accompanied me on foot along with our child from Tawang to Lumla, Bletting, Zimithang, Khinzemane and Bumla and helped me filling up, the pages of my diary and has contributed in all possible way in my effort. I am grateful to her.

After compiling the script the problem was to give a title to the book. This was solved by my friend Shri Tsering Gyurme, now cabinet minister in Arunachal Pradesh Government. He suggested the title "MONYUL" – The land of Monpas. During 15th century the second Dalai Lama Gendun Gyasto (1475-1543) after ordaining Lama hood to Monpa youth Tanpei Dronme, had directed him to proceed to Lhou-Mon" i.e. lower area to South of Tibet to propagate Gelugpa sect of Buddhism. Lhou-Mon became MONYUL.

Due to Scant leisure of a busy official life, the backward state of my own knowledge on many points, I have not been able to make the book more presentable. I hope to be excused for the crudeness of treatment and errors which are present in the book. But if this book, notwithstanding its shortcomings, prove of some use to those seeking information on the people, terrain, religion and customs of west Kameng, Tawang and East Kameng districts, I shall feel amply rewarded for all my labourers.

101 Shivkunj

Gandhi Nagar, Boring Road, Patna-1,

Email:- jspsingh1503@gmail.com

J.S.P. Singh

CONTENTS

CHAPTER ONE

Arunachal Pradesh

India is an unique example of unity in diversity and Arunachal Pradesh itself is a storehouse of diversities. It consist of twenty four main tribes and about one hundred and two other sub-tribes with their own culture, language, dress and customs. Combined with these are the scenic beauty, different atmosphere, forestry and a variety of wild life. This land which is widely different from the rest of India, is certainly a place for anthropologists.

Situated in the north-east India, its snow clad mountains receive the first sun ray of the day hence is rightly called Arunachal Pradesh. Four big rivers-Kameng, Subansiri, Siang (Brahmaputra), Lohit rise from the Himalayan range and after passing through dense forests, pastures and habitats merges with Brahmputra in plains of Assam.

Arunachal Pradesh has an area of 3,570 Sq Km with 6,28,050 population according to 1981 census. On 20 january 1972 it was made union Territory from North-East frontier agency (NEFA). And hence forth a number of administrative reforms were made. The agency council of NEFA was changed to Pradesh council and its chief administrator who was also Adviser to the Governor of Assam was redisgnated as chief commissioner. In 1975 according to the 37th amendment of the constitution, this union territory was allowed to elect its own legislature and ministry. The chief commissioner became the Lt. Governor. Sri Raja whose contributions towards the developments of this region are many, was made the first Lt. Governor of Arunachal Pradesh.

Pradesh council was made into ad-hoc legislative assembly and its councilors and members were made into ad-hoc ministers and legislative member. Sri Pema Khandu Thungon, a councilor from kameng district became the first Chief minister. The administrative centre which upto 1974 was in shillong, was shifted to Naharlagun, a temproy base and the task of building a permanent capital at Itanagar, ten Kms. ahead of Naharlagun started.

On 20 February 1987 the fifteen year old U.T. was accorded the status of a full fledged state in a grand ceremony by the then Prime minister Sri Rajiv Gandhi.

Till recently transport and communication facilities being non- descript and antiquated as well as to a lesser extent due to the inner line permit inforce, the state was less known than the rest of the country. But with the construction of good all weather roads and the advent of the state transport corporation buses plying on these roads these facilites have improved considerably though the inner line permit still exists in a much more relaxed way. And can be obtained without much hassle from the liaison officers at Delhi, Kolkata, Guahati, Mohanbari, Tezpur, Itanagar and Lilabari.

Prior to its being declared an U.T. NEFA had five frontier divisions kameng, Subansiri, Siang, Lohit and Tirap. Arunchal Pradesh now has eleven districts. Moving from west to east these districts with their headquarters are Tawang HQ Tawang, West Kameng Bombila, East Kameng -Seppa, Lower subansiri - Zero, Upper Subansiri-Daporijo, West siang-Along,

East siang- Pasighat, Dibang- Anini, Lohit-TEZU, Tirap-Khonsa and Changlang.

The Northern borders of Kameng division starts from Indo- Tibbet-Bhutan trijunaction (alt-17243') and runs eastward over the Thangla mountain ranges (alt-13263'-17059') and crosses the Namjangchu near Khinjemane. Still continuing its run towards east it hinges atop the Thongdrong and Jangla, ridges moving south up to Chemo-karpo La, Karsang La, and Duire. From Duire it straightens out to east passing over Bum La, touches Nakchutpa mountain profile and bends to North-east crossing Tsona chu, DarkoRong, and then passes over Thangla and Shya La directly to the east.

Moving further unceasingly it crosses Gonkhar La in the north-east direction and Thulung La, in the north (alt. -19431') Khang La I (alt. 19350') Khang La -II (20659) Cherong La (21027') respectively in the east and then moves over the highest peaks in kameng- Gorichen(24450') Kongto (23260'), Nyethi Khangsang (23120') and ends at spot height 20950'.

The eastern boundary between kameng and Suabansiri division start from peak 20950 ft in the North to south-east over triangular heights 11320' and straight to south over unnamed mountain ranges making watersheds up to trig height 7200'. It takes a turn to east to the height of 7590' and then turn sharply to west over trig height 7290' and 6980'. From here the boundary line goes straight to south and ends in the foothills in Assam at Bhinari at the innerline limit.

The southern boundary starts from Bhinari and goes through Seijusa, Bhaluk pong, kamengabari and ends at Bhairav kund. The western side is the international boundary with Bhutan.

It starts from Bhairav kund in the south and follows the mountain ridges to north over triangular heights 7094', Nyerpa Gyamtsola 10020', Mesagoang, Dangeng La, Tasang che and joins Japtan Ree. Along the Japtan Ree the line goes to east upto the conflunence of Phutan Ree. From here the boundary runs to North-west over Water-sheds, mountain ridges, pastures to Baggajhang 14600'. From Bagga-Jhang to west over Neyensang La, Gotpi, Pun-sum, Chang-chongma to North Kharung che, After touching kharungche the line again goes to west over village Bongleng and dips to Tawang chu near Dongshing mang.

From the confluence of Tawangchu and Worong chu the boundry line goes to North-West towards Jangphu, Brohang La 11552, Mirgu La 12723', Jongping La 13000, Khaktang La 14000, Markang La 14000, Lumpu La, Sumdo La and joins at the trijunction of India Bhutan and Tibbet.

The habitation in Kameng is mostly in the villages. The monpa inhabitants of Tawang chu and Namjang chu valleys are called "Brahmi" and of Dirang and Nargon chu valley "Tsangle". The people of Bichom River valley are Miji and Akas, The Sherdukpen and Buguns inhabitate the Tenga River valley. In east kameng in the main valley of kameng River and its tributaries Bangnee and Sulungs live. Brahmi, Tsangle and sherdukpen are Budhist while there is a superficial influence of Budhism and vaishnvism of Assam on Aka, Miji and Buguns. Mainly they are worshippers of Nature. The Bangnee and Sulungs are animists.

As per 1981 census the population of Dirang Monpa is 10,062 Tawang Monpa 18,662 Kalaktang Monpa- 2100, sherdukpen 2007, Aka-2301, Miji -2602, and Buguns-493. The population of Bangnee and Sulungs as per 1971 census is 24471 and 2808 respectively.

CHAPTER TWO

Blue Hills

Kameng district is bounded by Bhutan in the west, Subansiri in the East, Tibet in the North and Assam in the South. Nearest railway station to this place are Rangapara north and Tezpur. Sixty Kms from Tezpur is Bhalukpong from where the Inner line starts. A new railway line is being constructed from Rangapara north to Bhalukpong. The sixty kms long road lies in the plains of Assam, and passes through dens forests of sal, along the Bharali (Kameng) river. From Bhalukpong, which is at a height of 213 meters, a 100 Kms long road goes to Bomdila, through hilly terrain and verdant forest. It reaches Nechiphu also called zero point, at a height of 1708 meters. Seppa, the district headquarters of East Kameng is situated at 99 Kms from Nechiphu.

An old folk lore of Bhalukpong goes to say that after Banasur and his sons were killed by Lord Krishna in a war their grandson, Bhaluk had taken refuge here. Bhaluk performed a big yajna over here to please the gods. The burnt rice in this yajna is still to be seen after extracting it from the ground 3 kms of Bhalukpong. Banasur has his capital at Soniptpur (Tezpur) on the hills of Agnigarh, beside the Brahmputra. It was here, where Usha, had kept Anirudh as her captive.

In Bhalukpong, beside the road there is a small pond and a small clump of yellow bamboos. This is a sacred place for the Aka tribes. Six kms from Bhalukpong, at Tippi, an orchidarium is established by the forest department, which is worth visiting. This is at a height of 1113 ft. Here 500 varieties of orchid, of the North East region are kept. Close to it, beside the kameng river is the forest departments Rest house.

From Bhalukpong upto NechiPhu there was no population. For twelve kms from Bhalukpong, the road goes along the kameng river and then the ascend on the hill starts. After crossing the height of 1708 Mtr at Nechi-phu, the road again descends to a small camp called Jamiri. All these region belongs to Aaka tribe. After jamiri, the road goes along the Tenga river called Diying Kho for 38 Kms and reaches Dahung and Tenga Bazar. Six Kms from Tenga bazaar the road bifurcates to the left for Rupa. The right hand side road goes to Bomdila. From here the 12Kms long ascend to Bomdila starts.

After 6Kms from jamiri, area of the Bugun (khawa) tribes starts. Dahung, Tenga Bazar area, which ones belonged to Bugun village Sinchung, is now occupied by military camp. Local name for Tenga is Jalyap, and for Tenga river is Giding kho. At the confluence of Dukhang Nala and Tenga river, the region of Bugun tribe ends. From here the western and southern area belongs to sherdukpen tribes and the north-east region is clained by the Bugun's.

Bomdila was established in 1952 as the headquarter of Kameng by the then political officer, Shri Ralengnau Khating M.C., M.B.E. of Indian Frontier Administrative Service. From 1965 to 1967, I had the opportunity of serving under shri Khating. In one of our informal talks, Shri Khating had mentioned that upto 1951 the kamenga frontier was governed from Charduar in Assam. After being appointed as Assistant political officer of Tawang, he was on the look out for a place from where the kameng frontier Division could be better administered. In those days, one had to walk from Charduar, Missamari, Foot hills, Doimara, Chaku, Pirila, Jabrang and Rupa to reach this place.

On the way from Rupa to Bomdila, one had to cross two small hills and then walk up along the stream that came down from Bomdila. Bomdila, then had thick forests of cane, pine, Rhodendrons, Bamboo and Titachap. From Kakaling, the way meandered to present craft centre and then to the Deputy Commissioner's bungalow; Here in place of craft centre and the government garrage below it, there were two big ponds. Also, there were five other small ponds in the area.

From the camp, the path led upwards to the present TV tower, from where it again descended to 9 Kms. From here one path goes towards Dirang and Tawang, after crossing Rahung village and another path led towards But, Nafra, Janachang. Khazalang. Liyak, Lapuk, Bameng and seppa of East Kameng.

To reach the region of the Monpa's and Miji tribe, one had to cross the 9000 ft high Bomdila pass. It was for this centeralized situation of Bomdila, that Shri Khating selected the southern slopes of Bomdila ridge as the headquarter. Roads were not built then. In 1965 shri khating was the security commissioner at Tezapur. It was then that I with a company of S.S.B. marched on foot along this old track. Though roads were constructed from foot hills to Bomdila and from Bhalukpong to Bomdila but to get a thorough idea of the area and also to get accustomed to the height, we were asked to march on foot by commandant Shri Janak kumar

LP.S. From Salonibari to the foot hills marching on plains was easy.

First night we halted on the banks of the river Belsiri. After the foot hills our climb had begun. Next day we reached Doimara, which is a developing village now. In those days it used to be the temporary winter abode of the Sherdukpens of Rupa. The 117 men of the company began to make preparations to spend the night on the banks of the Belsiri river at Doimara. Some went fishing in the river. I was also occupied in making a bed of green leaves for myself under a tree, when our Hav.Maj I. Muthaiyaa apporoched beaming with smile and asked if I would like to eat. On being questioned what it was to be eaten, he said something in Telgu which was beyond me to understand. He then tried to explain to me in English saying -sir, two legs, six cuttings, water slow! They had caught some crabs and he didn't know either its English or Hindi name. That night we had a good night sleep after a bawl of crab's soup. The climb from Doimara to chaku via Piri La was very steep. Those who had not maintained a reasonable balance between their needs and mobility and were carrying heavy pack, started throwing there unnecessary items in the forest to lighten their packs

After crossing Pirila (2829 mtr) the track descends to Jabrang (2516 mtr) and goes along the slops of the hill. At that time there was a small C.G.I. sheet roof staging hut at Jabrang, which is demolished now. From Jabrang the track comes down to village Thongre(1680 mtr). We halted for the night here, Thongre, is a Sherdukpen village. We called on the village headman called "Thik-Khau" who welcomed us with the traditional scarf-Khada and their home brewed beer-Phak.

Sherdukpen are Budhists and comparatively progressive tribe. Their nine villages are in the region south-west of

Bomdila. Rupa and Shergaon are the two large villages, having two hundred houses each. Remaining seven Thongre, Jigaon. Mingmachur, Jamiam, Dikshi, Chholyapam and Brokyulag are comparatively smaller. Sherdukpen have different clans like-Thungduk, Thungon, Khrime, Thongchi, Dinglyo, Mosobi and Megeji.

Next day we started very early in the morning and by eight we were climbing the Bomdila ridge. In 1965, Bomdila had only log cabins and Bamboo Bashas. The political officers office was at the site of present police station. There was no market or hotel here then. On reaching Bomdila Pass our sherdukpen and monpa men lighted agarbatti and shouted "Lhaso-Lo." After that they cried three times "Ayee-Ho- Hee" On enquiry they explained that at these high passes Angels and Demons both dwell. We burn the incense stick and offer a piece of stone on the already high pile of stone by the side of the track to please the Angels.

To ward of the demons we cry "Ayee-ho-hee" three times. After crossing Bomdila we followed the road up to 9 Kms, and then descended to village Rahung. We halted at village - Rahung for Lunch. The villager offered us plenty of their homemade fermented drink - Chhang and distilled hard licquor -"Arak"

The track started upward and reached village Dirang Dzong. We were received by a prominent villager shri Namtsering. He offered all of us salted tea, chang and Ara. After an hour rest we started for Dirang-Doom, Six Kms from Dirang Dzong. Dirang Doom is the administrative centre of this area.

We established our camp this side of Dirang river. Across the river there were about ten log and Bamboo bashas only, and the office of the circle officer. There was nothing this side of the river where we had camped. In due course this temporary camp became the permanent headquarter of S.S.B.

Young belle of Kameng.
L to R-Bugun, Bangnee, Migi, Aka,
Sitting- Dirang MonPa and Tawang MonPa

Sherdukpen woman

Bugun woman with child

CHAPTER THREE

Budhism in Monpa Area

The display of prayer flags, colored paper strips tied to the bushes and white washed "MANE" attracts one's attention as soon as one reaches Sherdukpen and Monpa village. At the entrance of the village one finds a gate made of stone and timber of which the ceiling is colorfully painted with Bhudhist icons. These gates are called "Kakaling". In the centre of the village or at some prominent place the village Gompa is situated.

Every Sherdukpen and Monpa house will have its worshipping altar on which photographs or idols of Budha and Guru Padamshambhav are placed. Also at some houses are found other idols painted green and black and depicting demonic faces with crown of human skulls. On the alter bowls of water, grains and Tsampa are put as offerings. Almost every month people observe some festive worshipping in which plenty of chhang, Arak, Non-Vegetarian meals are served. These are also permitted inside the Gompa but Smoking inside the Gompa is strictly prohibited. To understand this form of Budhism and method of worshipping, it became essential to learn the history of Budhism in this area.

The first Preaching of Loard Budha was at Sarnath in sixth century B.C. Emperor Ashok declared Budhism as state religion. During the region of Ashok a large number of

Budhist monks and Nuns were sent out of India to propogate Budhism. The common language of that era was Pali. Lord Budha also preached in Pali. Budhism spread to Nepal, Afghanistan, Kashmir, Mangolia, China, Thailand, Burma, Japan and Sri Lanka.

Upto seventh century A.D.Tibet had neither any religion nor any script. People lived in barbaric condition. During 620 to 650 AD king Songchen Gombu ruled over Tibet. He married Princess Bhrikuti of king of Nepal Anshu Barman of Newar dynasty. In the year 641 AD the Tibetan king married Princess Weng Chung Kung Chu of china. Both these princesses were initiated in Budhism and with their influence Budhism was propogated in Tibet. Both these princesses are worshipped in Gompas as incarnation of Goddess TARA. The Nepali Princess is depicted as "Green - Tara" and the Chinese princess as "White- Tara", King Songechen Gombu is considered incarnaton of Bhodhistava and worshiped as "chen - Reji" and patron God of Tibet.

King Songchen Gombu had sent his young minister Thonmi Shambhot along with a group of intelligent young men to India for studying in Nalanda University. Thonmi Shambhot and his group Studied at Nalanda under Pandit Deovidya Singh who was a scholar of not only Sanskrit and Pali literature but also of Budhist philosophy and literature.

Thonmi Shambhot on return to Tibet invented Tibetan Script based on Devnagri script. He also wrote a grammar for Tibtan language containing eight chapters.

At that time Tibet was under influence of Bon religion. People were worshipping natural forces like mountains, rivers, forests. Animal sacrifice was prevalent.

On propogation of Budhism the Bon Worshipping rites gradually were abandoned. But it seems that wherever Budhism was propogated, the preachers did not take a very rigid attitude. Prevaling local rites and customs wherever found compatible to tenents of Budhism were incorported in Budhist rites and were not forbidden. Only animal sacrifices were totally banned. The monks preaching Buddhism were considerate and alert to the fact that Budhism should become untenable to the laity.

The translations of books on Budhism were taken up on grand scale after the development of Tibetan script. Scholars in large numbers were assigned to this task. They were called Lho Chhan-BA and Lho- BAN.

In the beginning of 8th century two prominent scholars visited Tibet from India. One was SANTRAKHIST an inhabitant of Gaur region of Bengal and Professor of Nalanda University. The other also from Udayan region of Bengal and a great tantrik Achary Guru Padamshambhaw. After a few years the third Scholar from India Kamlashil visited Tibet.

In due course Budhism devided into Hinyan and Mahayan. Hinyan proliferated in southern countries and preserved the canons and rites of Budhism as it was. Mahayan proliferated in Northen countries. Gradually Tantra, Mantra, Mudra, Mandala and mysticism got included in the Mahayana. The credit for all these goes directly to Guru Padamashambhawa. Guru Padam- shambhawa holds the same high spiritual position in Tibet, Bhutan, Sikkim and Monpa region as Lord Budha himself. He is called Guru Rimpoche, Lopon Rimpoche and Lopon Pema Jungme. Rimpoche means the precious one.

In the year 1042 one more prominent Scholar from India Atish Dipankar visited Tibbet. Atish Dipankar was second Son of king Klyanshri of Bengal. He was born in 980 AD. From the very childhood he exhibited signs of becoming a great Yogi. He was innunciated in Tantra by his father king Kalyanshri. He renunciated the royal privileges and spent his life in preaching and propagating Budhism. He was made Chancellor of Vikramshila University in 1038 AD.

During that time king Ralpachen was ruling Tibbet. He invited a number of Scholors from India. Prominent among them who visited Tibbet were Jinmitra, Sailendra Bodhi, Surendra Bodhi, Pragya Barman, Danshil and Bodhi Mitra. King Ralpachen requested them to translate the Sanskrit and Pali text on Budhism and other subjects in Tibbetan language. He also granted land and authority to collect tax to the Budhist Gompas. King Ralpachen died in the year 899 and his brother Lungderma became king.

King Lungderma put a ban on Budhism and prosecuted Budhist monks. He wanted to revive the old practices of Bon religion.

The local myth about king Langdarma is very interesting. It is said that Langdarma had horns on his head. He used to hide his horns under long hairs and in a long cap. Every week a young female was deputed for dressing of his hair and was killed on the orders of Langdarma so that his having horns on the head is not divulged to others. Once the young girl who was sent for this task started weeping and her tears fell on the hands of Langdarma. When asked why she is weeping, the girl told him this is the last day of her life as there is a precedence of execution after she has completed the Job of hair- dressing. Langdarma was moved and spared the life of the girl on the promise that she will not divulge this secret to any one. The girl promised and saved her life. After a few days this knowledge became unbearable to the girl and she had a compelling urge to divulge this secret to some one lest she will go mad. Therefore she took a hollow bamboo piece and putting her mouth in this hollow tube spoke in river water that king Langdarma has got horns on his head. The winds carried these words to Lama Palgay Dorgee. Lama Palgay Dorgee dressed himself in a long headgear and cape with wide and long sleeves. Inside his long sleeves he concealed a bow and arrow. He got his white pony painted black. He came near the royal palace and started a devil dance. The news went to king Langdarma that an amazing devil dance is being performed under his palace balcony. He came to watch the performance. Lama Palgay Dorgee at an opportune moment took out his bow and arrow and shot king Langdarma. Lama Palgay Dorgee after killing Langdarma escaped crossing the river during which the black paint of his pony washed away and the pony became white again. This deceived the soldiers following him. Today also during Torgay festival this is enacted at Tawang monastry.

According to another myth of the Monpa when Santrakshit commenced porpogation of Budhism in Tibet the demonic and evil spirits got enraged and caused flood and Thunder. This was followed by famine. The priests and followers of Bonism blamed santrakshit for bringing all these natural calmities. At that time Guru Padamshambav was residing in Nepal.

Shantrakshit is addressed as "Khanchin Bodhisatwa" and "Palden Jiwachho" in Tibetan books. Santrakshit invited Guru Padam Sambhav from Nepal. Guru Padam Shambhav on his arrival eliminated all Ghosts and Demons exercising his power of Mantra. Some of the demons surrendered before

Guru Padamsambhaw. They vowed to act as protectors of the people and Budhism. On their begging Guru Padamsambhav granted them amnesty and allowed their placing and worshiping in Gompa.

The influence of the great preceptor Guru Padamshambhaw widely added propogation of Budhism in Tibet. His sermons and doctrines were recorded in Tibetan language. All these written records were divided in to two categories. The canons of Budhism were written in 108 volumes and called "Kangyur".

Each volume of Kangyur is cf about 1000 pages comprising of 1083 distinct words. The size is 26"X 8"X8" and weight 4 to 5 kilograms. Kangyur is devided in to three prominent sections the Tripitika corresponding to the three volume of Pali Tripitika.

1. The DUL-VA (Sanskrit-Vinaya) is 13 volumes. Compiled by UPALI
2. The Do (Sanskrit- SUTRA) in 66 volumes compiled by Anand inclusive of Tantra.
3. The CHOS-NON-PA (Sanskrit-Abhidharma) is 21 volumes complied by Maha Kashyap. It contains Trancedental wisdom (Tibatan - SER- CHIN Sanskrit - Pragyaparamita)

The Do or sutra sections has been devided in to eight further volumes making total of 108 volumes.

The SER-CHIN (Pragya parmita) 21 vols are compilation of Budha's latest recollection in his discourse at Gridhkut, Rajgrih. The first 12 volumes are called BUM (Skt- Sat Sahasrika) the 10,000 Shloks of transcedental wisdom.

Another 3 vols are called NYi-Thi with 20,000 slokas. The abridged versions of kangyur are Dobangs and Dorchhoi.

The other category called Tangyur is a great encyclopedia. It is compilation of all sorts of literary works written mostly by ancient Indian scholars like Ashwaghosh, Nagarjun, Asang, Vasubandhu and Atish Dipankar. It also contains writing of some Tibetan scholars in the first few centuries after the introduction of Budhism in to Tibet commencing with the seventh century of our era. The whole makes 225 volumes. Out of these 225 volumes 130 volumes are said to be written by Atish Dipankar. These volumes are divided in to two classes - Gyud and Do i.e. Tantra and Sutra.

The Gyud 87 volumes are on tantrik rituals and ceremonies. The Do on sciences and literature are in 136 volumes. The first 16 volume of Do are all commentaries on PRAGYAPARAMITA, other several volumes explain the Madhyamika Philosophy of Nagarjuna. One separate contains hymns and prayers on several deities and saints. One volume is the index for Whole. Another volume contains Tibeto - Sanskrit dictionary of Budhist terminology. It is called JE-TAK-TU-JOG-JE. Atish Dipankar also translated Sanskrit text on Tantra in to Tibetan. He further wrote his own doctrine on kalchakr Tantrik rite.

Mean while the influence of Lamaism gained strength in Mahayan. The introduction of wine, meat, fish, mudra etc only for some tantrik rites by guru Padamshmbhav were taken in their daily life by the Lamas. Atish Dipankar brought reform in the principles of Lamaism and propogated a new sect called Kadmpa The followers of old Lamaism called themselves Ningmapa. In course of time further reforms were introduced in kadampa and it acquired a new name GELUGPA. The lamas of this sect adopted yellow cap for rituals. The Ningmapas adopted red cap The head of GELUGPA sect became the Dalai Lama. Besides these a number of other sects and sub-sects came up. Atish Dipankar left this world at the age of 73 in the year 1054 at Lhasa.

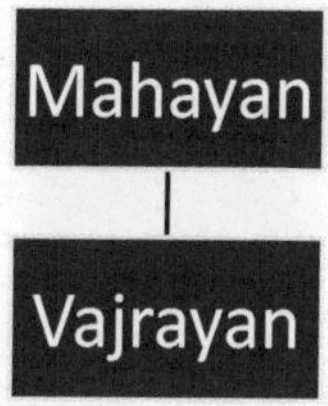

Chief Propogator-NAGARJUN (Tibetan-Gombu LUTUP). He propogated the doctrine of void in his MADHYAMIK Philosophy. The last propgater of this doctrine was Dharamkriti in the seventh century, By eleventh Century four promineant sects came up.

Four Prominent Sects-

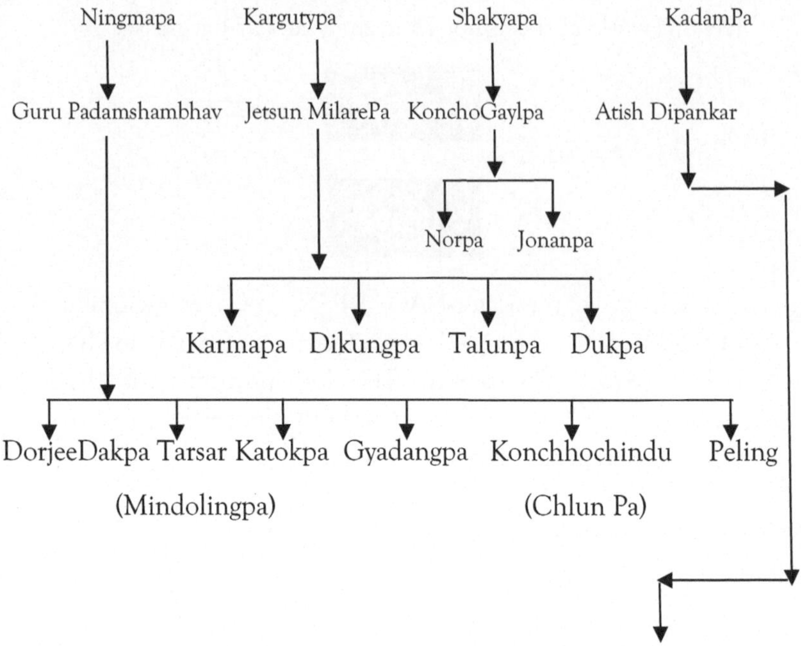

Lobjang Drakpa (1356-1418) named it Gelugpa. He was born in Amdo area of Tibet in Chongkhpa region and is also Known as Chongkhapa. In MONPA area he is addressed as JERINPOCHE. IN 1409 he established Galden Monastery. Followers are called Gelugpa (Followers of virtuous order)

Budhism came to Monpa and Sherdukpen region of Arunchal Pradesh from India via Nepal. The religious and cultural bond of Arunchal Pradesh with the main land is as old as the mountains and forests of the region. The difference between Ningmapa and as explained by the local Lamas are

Ningmpa	**Gelugpa**
1. Lamas wear red cap	1. Lamas wear yellow cap
2. The main statue in Gompas is Guru Padamshambhav	2. The main Statue in Gonpa of ChongkhaPa
3. The rules of Celebacy for Lama not essential.	3. Lamas must follow celibacy and 223 other rules of conduct.
4. Tutelary diety -KUNTO NANGPO SAMANTABHADRA)	4. Tutelary diety- DORJEE CHANG (Adi -Budha- VAJARADHARA)

Both these sects preserve and study Kangyur and Tangyur and believe in re incarnation. Most of the Lama of KargytutPa and Shakypa sects also follow celibacy. Those who do not follow the rules of Celebacy are not granted the title of "Geshi" and "Tulku". Even in Ningmapa sects celibate Lamas are given higher respect. They are devided in two classes RABYUNG - celebate hermit and Nangpa- Tantrik. The NangPa are allowed to marry and lead family life.

CHAPTER FOUR

Om Mane Peme Hum

The Monpas and Sherdukpens recite this prayer at all times. On the mountain tracks at intervals by the side of the path are found whitewashed stone walls and resting places. These are called MANE. The MANE is decorated with painted or engraved stone slabs of the prayer Om MANE PEME HUM in different colours. While climbing the steep mountain path this prayer is chanted spontaneously by the Monpa companions and we also started chanting this prayer. But the meaning and mysticism of this "Mantra" was explained to me by my colleague Sri Pema Wangchuk, a Budhist officer, belonging to kalimpong. We had been going together on tour to distant places in kameng Frontier division. His morning rituals used to start with the incantation of Om Mane Peme Hum. Sri Wangchuk explained to me that this is the "BIJ- MANTRA" of ChenRejig. (Avalokiteshwar). It is addressed to the patron God of GelugPa who is the Controller of rebirth and Moksha. According to book "MANE-KAH-BUM" this prayer can bestow happiness, prosperity and knowledge. Even the very sighting of the painted and engraved mantra on Mane is beneficial to all humane beings. Therefore this mantra is written on prayer flags, prayer-wheels and MANE walls. The root mantra is Om Amogh Vairochan Mahamudra Mani Padama Jwala Pravaty HUM. Prior to this mantra the Bon religion Mantra "DZU" was prevalent. MATRI MUTRI SA LA.

It is stated that OM closes the door of rebirth amongst God, MA amongst Titan (Asur), Ni amongst human, PAD amongst beast, ME amongst Tantalus (Pret) and Hum as inhabitant of hell. These words are painted in specified colours - Om in white. Ma in Blue, Ni in yellow, PE in Green, ME in red and Hum in Black.

The history of Gelugpa sect in Monpa and Sherdukpen area was narrated by different lamas on our visit and stay in their Gompa. The history started with the story of Tibatan Lama Thang Ton GyalPo. Lama Thang Ton Gyalpo is also called Thongstan Gyalpo by some narrators. He was contermporary to the first Dalai Lama Genden Drub (1391-1475 AD). In the Monpa village Gompa his image is found on wall paintings. He was a religious preacher as well as an engineer. He got constructed a bridge on river Tawang Chu to connect the villages kitpi and Mukto. The bridge is made of iron Chain link. It is called Chaksam and still existing.

Lama Thangton Gyalpo meditated in Changkhargor cave twelve Kms south-east of village Kraling. On completion of his meditation he came to village - Barkhar and gave his begging bowl full of "Arak" to a villager named Barkhar Targey. He instructed him that if he will keep this sacred bowl well preserved at a sacred place, he will be blessed with seven talented brave and courageous sons. With the blessings of Lama Thangton GyalPo Seven Sons were born to Barkhar Targey. They were called PAUDUN. (PAU- Brave and strong DUN- seven). The second and seventh sons Tanpie Dronme and Lobsang Khichung became Lama. They were initiated and later educated by Changton Hrolpi Dorjee, a prominent teacher under the first DalaiLama.

The Second Dalai Lama Gendun Gyatso (1475- 1543 AD) himself initiated Tanpie Dronme by shaving his head and made him Galong. The real monk.

Any new entrant to Lamaism is first taken as Geyen - the lay brother. Then he becomes Getsul- underpriest or Deacon and is bound to follow the Thirtysix rules of conduct. From Getsul One Graduates to Galong the real monk and has to observe 253 rules of conduct.

The Galong becomes K'an Po - Abbot in due coarse. Only after attaining the grade of Galong One becomes eligible to study the mystic mantras and rites of Tantra practices.

The name TanPie Dronme was also given by the second Dalai Lama and he instructed him to travel to LHOU- MON (LHOU -South MON-lowerland) and propogate GelugPa sect among the MONPAS i.e. the inhabitants of lower land. The second Dalai Lama also advised him to visit Assam and cultivate friendhip with the then King of Assam.

Tanpie Dronme on coming to Monpa region got constructed the first Gompa over village -LHOU under a steep standing white rock, called BARAKAR Gompa. (BRAH-Mountain. KAR- White). The white rock is visible from a distance. During his stay in this region he desired to construct another Gompa at a sacred location. One day he filled his begging bowl with consecrated water and threw the bowl with his Tantrik power in the air. The begging bowl landed at a distance of two Km at ARAIKDUN. The Consecrated water was as it is in the bowl. The second Gompa was constructed at ARAIKDUN. The third Gompa constructed by him is six Km east of Tawang at Lhanghatin. The maintenance of these three Gompas are given to the seven villages of this area - BARKHAR, SAMKHAR, SHERNUP, GRANGKHAR,

KHARTUNG, LHAH ARAGON and KISHUNG. These seven villages pay "DRUFUI" to these GomPa every year.

The fourth and fifth Gompa constructed by Lama Tanpie Dronme SANGLAMPHE and TANDUNG and were given to villages BAMBA and BUMTENG for maintenance. He further got constructed TAIDUNG Gompa at village - Thongleng, SURCHUNG Gompa at village Lumla and TASHICHOLENG Gompa in SAKTEN area of Bhutan. In compliance to the instruction of the second Dalai Lama, TanPie Dronme visited Assam and called on the then king of Assam. He was accorded proper respect there and the king granted him a large tract of land at Udalgiri and Amar Tola. Among the last construction work of Tanpie Dronme are DUNGSUM and GALDEN CHHOLING GomPa in village. MERA in Bhutan. TanPie Dronme expired at the age of 99 years in GALDEN CHHOLING gompa.

The incarnations of Lama TanPie Dronme further expounded GelugPa sect in Monpa area. Such incarnations represented Bodhisatva in humane form who voluntarily accept re-birth on this earth to propogate the religion and assist people to attain MOKSHA from this world.

The craving of the religious minded populace for a living God is fulfilled by these incarnations, the images of manifestations of different Bodhisatawa, the lamas and other symbols Painted or carved on wood and stones. In the houses the alter called CHHOSUM represents the mini gompa. In front of the statue of Lord Budha are kept Silver, brass and copper lamps of Yak butter. On the altar are also kept bowls of these metal bowls full of water. The water is changed every morning. Such bowls are usually seven or even more. The Monpas believe that the water collected form the river or stream comes from the high mountains and are sacred.

By the side of the altar are found cloth hangings of beautiful paintings depicting different figures of deities. The sherdukpens call it KUTHANG and the Monpas CHEDANG. In prosperous houses we found three, four or even five KUTHANG. These five KUTHANG are described as:-

i. CHANTONG CHANGTONG KUTHANG on this are painted CHEN REJI-Avalokiteshwar with Thousand arms and eyes.

ii. TUNGSHAK KUTHANG Paintings of thirtyfive manifestations of Loard Budha.

iii. LOPON KUTHANG Eight manifestation of Guru Padamshamhav. These eight forms are - Guru Pemajungme, guru nyipa ujer, guru shakya senge, guru loden choksi, guru senge dhadho, guru pema gyalpo, guru chhokyi dorjee and guru dorji trolho.

iv. CHEPA ME KUTHANG- Lord Budha.

v. AMITAYU JIGJE KUTHANG - The ferocious face of Jigje (VAJRA BHAIRAV) with two horns on his head, in blue colour having a female consort in embrace is depicted. Beneath it is painted the miniature of demons and above it the mild benevolent faces of gods and goddess.

Outside the houses are made small incinerator called SANGPHUM. In this are burned the leaves of Juniper, the smoke of which spreads its mild perfume in the atmosphere every morning. On the other side of the house front is the MANE. It is a wooden prayer wheel on which is painted OM MANE PADME HUM. In side this wooden cylinder are kept long strips of paper on which are written prayers and mantras. The prayer wheel is on an iron axis. Members of the house turn the wheels while going out or coming in the house, with their right hand. It is believed that turning of these prayer wheels bestows on them the same benefit as of reading the prayers and mantras kept in the prayer wheel.

Other type of MANE is constructed with stone and mortar by the side of the tracks. The smallest size of these walls are six feet in length and the largest size found of approximately fifty feet. The height of these MANES at every place is approximately seven feet. These are constructed on the outskirts of the villages, on the steep climbing paths at some distances at suitable places where people walking on these Paths can take rest. On both end of these MANES are found the prayer wheels. On the MANE in the niche are kept rectangular or square small stone slabs on which are either engraved or painted OM MANE PEMA HUM, JAMPEYANG (MANJUSHREE), CHEN-REJIG (AVALOKITESHWAR) CHHANA DORJEE (VAJRAPANI) and the mystic monogram of NAMCHHU WANG DEN. The local custom is to pass from left of these MANES so that it is always at your right side.

Like these mane, ones attention is attracted to the CHORTEN (STUPA) small and large near the villages. These are constructed as memorial to the late lamas and prominent people of the village after their death. These CHORTEN contains the remnant of the dead person and called KUDUNG. In those CHORTEN in which are kept some item of their personal use are called DUNGTEN. These chortens are built with the belief that their soul will have a noble rebirth. A number of chorten are built jointly by the villagers and in these chorten they keep the religious text and idols. These are built for the prosperity and well being of the

the village. Small miniature chorten of terracota, brass and copper are also made and offered in the Gompa.

Chorten is the symbolic structures of Budhist period "CHAITYA" and "STUPA". They were built to preserve the sacred memorials. To day also they are built with the same belief and reverence. On rectangular or square platforms are constructed a dome which in the commonest form is inverted. This is the Sanctorum (GARBHA) in which sacred texts and idols are kept. On this is erected a square TORAN. The width of the Toran is less than the upper part and from the angel of Indian Vastu - Art it looks inverted. On the Toran is a pyramedical spire -CHOORAMANI of steps like segments. These are thirteen in number and symbolic of thirteen Bodhistava heaven. This is surmounted by a bell shaped symbol usually copper-gilt called KALASH. Above it a lotus flower or crescent moon, a globular sun, surmounted by a tongue shaped spike representing the Jyoti of Budha. At some places above around the Kalash a gilt or wooden canopy is also made. Chorten is also symbolic of the five elements in which body is dessolved upon death. The lowest section a solid rectangular block is the solidity of earth; above it water is represented by a globe, fire by a triangular tongue, air by a crescent, inverted vault of the sky and ether by an acuminated circle the tapering in to space.

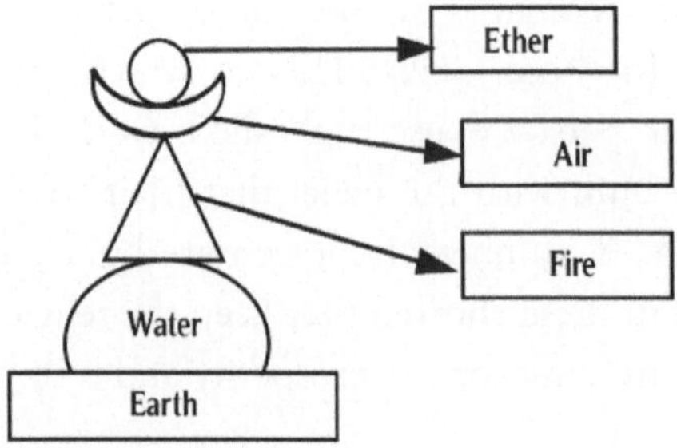

Construction of MANE and CHORTEN is a pious deed. They satisfy their religious belief and are symbolic of their religious faith.

Another such act along with other religious rites is putting prayer flags called PHAN. On their new years LOSAR colored flags are put on the roof of all Monpa and Sherdukpen houses. One in the front and other in the back. These flags are connected with a string and on the string small colored paper flags are tied in a row. In front of the houses, Gompa and at fixed places on the hills long flag poles are put. The cloth flag, on these poles are 12 to 18 inches in width and ten to twelve feet in length. On these cloth flags are printed prayers and mantras with wooden mould. These printed flags are called LUNGPHAN or DUMPHAN. The plain flags are called CHEPHAN. The flags on the long poles are also called DARSING and on small poles LUNGTOH. After the death of a family member rites of SHARDH is performed and for the peace of the departed soul such flags are put in front of the Gompa.

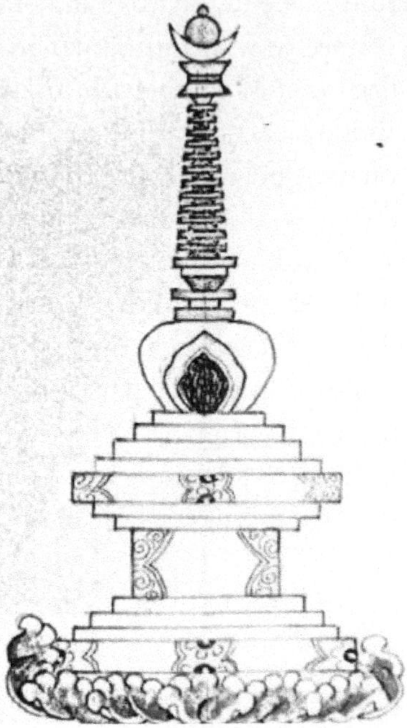

Chorten (Stupa)

CHAPTER FIVE

Chhoksum

Today's TAWANG, according to ancient folk lore of this area was called CHHOKSUM. Three incarnations of Terton Lama Pema LingPa Came to this area as three brothers. The first brother found a golden plough near village SERU. He took it as an auspicious symbol, a devine blessing and developed this area. The area was called SERU -CHHAK means Golden - area.

The second brother moved ahead and climbing on a hill surveyed the area ahead for a suitable landscape. He sighted three maidens weaving cloth at a far distance. When he reached there, the three maidens vanished. He came back to the same hill. From the hill again he sighted those three maidens. This time he took a thread from his clothes, consecrated it with power of mantra and shot it with his arrow towards them. The arrow passed touching the head of one of the maiden. When he came to the place he found that maiden while the two others had vanished. He married the young girl and developed that area as SHEYAR -CHHOK.

The third brother with his own ability and strength developed LHOU - CHHOK. The group of SERU-CHHOK, SHEYAR CHHOK and LHOU- CHHOK was called CHHOK - SUM the three Chhok.

Today SERU-CHOK Consist of the villages Seru, Muchut, Tilli, Khrimu, half of vill- Namet, Shorbi, Tengthin, Lhahargang, Bomja, ChangProng, Kangteng and the kidung meadow across the Kangteng stream.

Sheyar - Chhok has the villages - Bamba, Bumteng, ongar, Mayeedung, Gyangkhar, Paidar, Khartoot, Lebleyang, Changpu, Tamgen-Wangpu, other half of village - Namet, half of village -Bomdir and Gryangkhar.

Lhau Chhak consist of villages - Lhau, sheyaru, Jhang, - Mukto, Gongkhar, Gyamdong, kitpi, oudung, Jamkhar, Sonu, Khardung, watphung, Kraling, Broksar, Somang, Chaksam, and Khrimu.

The area across the the kangten stream is called Dakpa Chhogeyat i.e. the group of eight areas.

Lama TanPie Dronme's fourth in carnation was born in Paudoon family of Chhok-Sum and was called Lodro Gyatso. He was born in the family of one of the five brothers of Paudoon. Lodro Gyasto after completing his education in Lamaism as Geying, Getsul and Galong, went to Tibbet and graduated as Geshi from SERA and Guyeme monastsies. The ordination in Geshi is achieved after successful completion of the studies in mystic knowledge and rites. Only after obtaining the title of Geshi, a lama becomes eligible to be admitted to Guyeme and Guyete ocult centres. These centres were affliated with Galden monastery of Tibbet. Post Chinese occupation of Tibbet these centres are now functioning in India.

Lama Lodro Gyastso after obtaining his tantrik achievements returned to Bhutan from Tibbet. He made has permanent residence at Galdern Chholing monastery at Vill-Mera. Due to this he was popularly known as MERA LAMA.

During this time DUKPA sect gained prominence in Bhutan. The followers of DukPa sect started prosecuting the Gelugpas and even tried to anihilate Mera Lama. MeraLama left Bhutan and came to chhok sum. He resided in Sanglamphe Gompa. In this area also the influence of KarmaPa and NyingmaPa sects were prominent. When Mera Lama could not get any success, he returned to Tibbet. It was the regime of the 5th Dalai Lama Nawang Lobzang Gyatso (year 1616- 1682). The Dalailama after listening to the unsuccessful attempts of Mera Lama issued a sacred decree directing the inhabitants of Chhoksum to extend all help to MeraLama in his projects.

In Chhoksum during that Period there were thrce Gompas of Nyingma sects. Urgeling Gompa, 3 Kms south of present Tawang, Sangeling Gompa 2 Kms west of Urgeling and third ChhorgeLing Gompa 3Kms south-west. All the three Gompas were constructed by Lama Sherbum of Bhutan and were known as Lingsum. It is said that these three Gompas were constructed some time before 1177 A.D. At present only Urgeling and Sangeling Gompas are there. In the process of modernization of Tawang and construction of roads, Chhorgeling Gompa got destroyed. Sanglemphe and Tadung Gompas also met the same fate.

According to the folklore of the Lamas of Tawang Gompa Guru Padamsambhav recorded the mystic rites and concealed these in the caves and Lakes of this area for the future generations. These writings are called TERMA and those who were fortunate enough to find these are called TERTON. Lama PemalingPa of Bhutan recovered one such TERMA from the bottom of a lake and was called Terton Pema LingPa. Lama Sherbum who got the Lingsum Constructed was son of Lama Pema LingPa.

These Gompas were damaged during the period of 5th Dalai Lama when the struggle for supremacy between NingmaPa and GelugPa Sects were at the climax. The sixth Lama Chhangyang Gyatso was born at Tawang in the family of Ningma Lama of Urgeling Gompa. After this these Gompas were reconstructed. Now only two of them are at Tawang.

Mera Lama again came to chhoksum with a decree of 5th Dalai Lama. The 5th Dalai Lama gave him a ball of thread and said that the perimeter of a new Gompa to be constructed by Mera Lama in Chhoksum will be equal to the length of the thread in the ball.

Mera Lama on his arrival in Chhoksum stayed in Sanglamphe Gompa. He was worried about finding a suitable site for the new gompa. One day engrossed in this problem he had gone to the cave Brahmdochhung 5Kms north of Tawang. There leaving his pony outside he sat inside the cave in meditation to receive some devine inclination about a suitable site. After some time when he came out, he did not find his pony. The pony had never left him prior to this. Mera Lama followed the hoof mark of the Pony and came to a place Tana Mandekhang. Once upon a time the palace of King Galpo Kala Wang Pen of this area used to be at this site. Mera Lama found his pony at this site.

The way pony was found standing, it gave an indication to Mera Lama that this is the site where he should construct the Gompa. The pony was considered the medium of the devine wish and after this Chhoksum was called TAWANG (TA - Pony WANG - Blessing). The perimeter of the site found there was exactly of the measurement of the thread. The villages of Chhoksum shared the construction work of the Gompa among them, and construction was completed in a record time. Today also these villages carry out the annual maintenance and repair of the part of the Gompa contructed by them. The houses inside the premises of the Gompa were also constructed by the villagers. The ground floor of the Gompa was constructed by the villagers of Tawang and Lumla. The upper story was constructed by the villagers of Pangchen area. The Gompa is called -Tawang Galden Namgey Lhatse - the place selected by the blessing of the Pony.

On completion of his aim Mera Lama went to Tibet and prayed to 5th Dalai Lama to visit Tawang to consecrate the Gompa and establish the tutelary Goddess in the Gompa. Dalai Lama made the image of the tutelary goddess PALDEN LHAMU (SRIDEVI), a manifestation of goddess KALI on a cloth with his blood taken out from his nostril. He consecrated this cloth, put it in a copper tube, sealed the tube and gave it to Mera Lama for establishing in the shrine. This Gompa is stated to be completed some time in the year 1680.

The fifth Dalai Lama could not visit Tawang due to some unavoidable reasons. He gave his words to Mera Lama that he will come to Tawang as soon as he finds time. For the time being he gave an auspicious date and time for placing the copper tube containing the image of tutelary goddess in the shrine inside the Gompa and stated that he will consecrate this ceremony from the roof top of Potala palace of Lhasa. The enthronement of tutelary goddess Palden Lhamu by Mera Lama was carried out as per instructions of the 5th Dalai Lama. The 5th Dalai Lama left this world without fulfilling his words given to Mera Lama. It is said that he took birth in Tawang as sixth Dalai Lama to fulfill his promise given to Mera Lama. Sixth Dalai Lama was born to the couple Lama Tashi Tenzing and his wife Chhowang Lhamu in the year 1683.

It is said that the temperature of copper tube brought to Tawang from Lhasa by Mera Lama was maintained to the digree of body temperature of a bird till it was enthroned in the shrine. Mera Lama during his life kept this copper tube in a sealed silver casket and prohibited its taking out.

CHAPTER SIX

Tawang

The Dirang valley is 42 kms from Bomdila. Tawang is 139 Kms. from Dirang. Metalled road from Bomdila via Dirang goes to Tawang over SELA at the hight of 13714ft. Before SELA the last village is SENGE: The construction of road and military camps have changed the geography of this village. In 1965 November when frst time I stayed in this village for few days, I was overwhelmed by the tranquility of the place, the smell of juniper leaves smoke coming out from Sangphum in front of the houses in the morning, the lilting sound of the bells hanging from the neck of yaks, and the sheet of white fog rising from the valley in the noon. There was only one shop by the side of the road of Lama Sonam. The items of daily use, sweet and salted tea were available in this shop. Lama Sonam had come to India along with Dalia lama's entourage in 1959. He resided in the two rooms constructed behind the shop. He made me stay in one of these rooms. The wooden coat was covered with blanket of yak hair and over it was spread a large hide of bear. On this bed the sleepingbag was adequately warm and comfortable at this height of 8500ft in the month of November.

We were to despatch a platoon of S.S.B.to Luguthang via SELA, Keye LA, ZaziLa, and Jalung La. The GaonBura of village SENGE provided yak and porters. Before sunrise we moved out with our forty men, twenty yaks and ten porters. The pine and rhodendron forests remained behind as we gained height. At Sela there were rhodendron bushes and bare rocks only.

One of our SSB Jawan Kon Tsering belonging to village SENGE explained that SENGE means lion. The village is named SENGE because on viewing from the top the hillock on which the village is situated looks like a sitting lion. In SENGE village large double storeyed houses are construed with stone and pine timber. The construction seemed unique as no iron nails were used in the construction from bottom to top. Even the hinges of the doors were made by cutting grooves in the timber.

It took us four hours to reach SELA top. Every one of us were carrying pack weighing more than fifteen kg. On SELA the monpa Jawans offered agarbatti and shouted Lhaso -Lo. From SELA I along with five men took the track to Tawang. Rest of the men marched on the right hand track to keyela, On coming down from SELA one enters NURANANG valley (Nu-valley, RONG stream NANG-Inside). The foot track goes along the stream coming down from SELA lake. The motrable road also follows this stream to some distance and then makes sharp loops while descending. Upto 1971-72 the road was so uneven that walking on foot was more comfortable than the bumpy ride of a vehicle. On both side of the stream were tall trees of blue pine called "wangsing". In between were the Rhondendron bushes called "Tamasing". From July to September the bank of the stream and the meadows on the slopes have abundance of small vivid colour wild flowers. It was a real pleasure to walk on this track, rest whenever one desire, prepare the tea and enjoy the Pack - Lunch. This was much better than getting body ache from the bumpy ride of a vehicle. Now the road has considerably improved. Still the tracking on this valley has its own charm. While climbing from SENGE to SELA it took four hours. We came down to Nuranang Bridge in one hour. After taking rest and tea at the bridge we marched downward to village JHANG, and reached there in two hours. The Gaonbura received us with Khada, Chhang and Ara. We got a place in the Gompa, situated in the centre of the village, to spend the night. The conversation with the Gaonbura and other villagers continued till late night.

Next day we marched for Tawang. The distance form Jhang to Tawang is 39 Kms by motorable road. But after crossing the bridge on TawangChu we took the foot track and climbed to village LHOU. From LHOU after meeting the Gaonbura PEMGOMBU and accepting his hospitality we moved and reached Tawang by noon.

We had left Dirang with a curiosity to cross SELA and see Tawang monastery. But SELA was covered with thick fog and we could not have a glimpse of the gompa.

Another day also till we reached Tawang every thing was covered under a thick fog. Next day from our camp we could see for the first time towards south-west on the slope of a hill the fortress like white washed structure of Tawang monastery and to the east adjacent to the monastery SHEYO village of 40 houses.

After this whenever I came to Tawnag I did not fail to visit and roam around the Gompa. Gradually I became familiar with every idol, wall paintings, items of religious rites, the two ivory tusks, the utensils of the common kitchen of Lamas and the library. At that time the abbot of the monastery was Rigya Rimpoche Kesang Phuntso. His simplicity and benevolent face impressed every one. The irony was that he did not know Hindi and I was not conversant with either Tibbetan or Monpa Languages. Whatever formal talk we had, was through his secretary. Lama Danga helped me in obtaining the knowledge about monastery. Lama Danga was a monpa and very proficient in Painting, colouring the wooden masks and organizing different functions and rituals. It took me some time to understand his way of speaking Hindi. Lama is a honorific term equivalent to 'ARYA' of Buddhist period Sanskrit term.

Tawang is a beautiful place situated at a height of 9500 to 10000 ft. On 6th oct' 1984 with the effort of the then young minister Tshering Tashi and M.L.A. Karma wangchuk of Arunchal Pradesh Government, Tawang was declared a separate district. On 6th oct' 84 the young minister was addressing a large gathering of villagers, Govt. officers, employees and military personnel's. The modern gadgets like public address system, video camera and other cameras were there. Suddenly memory went eighteen years back when we celebrated the Republic Day 26th Jan' 1966 in this very ground. It was extremely cold with a light shower. A wooden cot served a dais. The Asst: Politcal officer Sri Katuk Lama unfurled the tri colour. There was no public address system, cameras and video camera. Near the dais was a line of Gaonburas doning the red coat, a few Govt. employees and SSB personnel. Sri Katuk Lama delivered a short speech partially in Hindi and in Tawang monpa dilect. The formal function ended with JaiHind.

After this formal function we were invited by the Gaonburas to come to their camps. The fringe of the ground was covered with canvas tents erected by the villagers who came to attend the function a day earlier. The official group led by Asst Political officer Sri Katuk Lama, Political Asst Sri GyamtsoLa and Sri Rinchin Dhondup Neyer pa La moved from one camp to another. Every village camp had wooden drums full of chang and Ara. We were offered these drinks in silver cups and bowls with so much politeness and respect that it became difficult not to accept them. In the ground after some time the mask dance AZI LHAMU commenced. The whole atmosphere was full of joyfull hilarious scene. The difference between officials and villagers was completely eliminated. The function ended with the dinner in the house of Sri Katuk Lama.

Tawang was then a sleepy village. From SSB camp the sight towards north of Geshi La and BUMPA La across the green small hills and the changing colour of morning sun rays on their bare rocks was very captivating. In winter these were covered in snow and the sunrays reflected the rainbow colours. Below these hills Khromtin Gompa standing lonely always made me inquisitive. To the east from the camp villages Namet and Khrimu and to the east-south the long range of SELA ridges were visible. To the south across Tawangchu, villages -Mukto, Merba, Gyamdong and khet were visible. Above these villages the three high peaks of chong -chongma looked inviting. I resolved to walk in these forests, climb the peaks, and visit the villages and Gompas on the first opportunity and I got several opportunities during my stay in this area from 1965 to 1972. To the west Tawang Gompa and Gyangong Ani Gompa always attracted our attention.

Tawang monastery gives an impression of a fortress situated on a high hill. In the background of the history of violent struggle between Dukpa and Gelugpa sects the situation of this monastery ought to have been at such site. The followers of Dukpa sects made several attacks to capture

Tawang. Mera Lama gave due consideration to this aspect in construction of the Gompa. The deep ravine to the west of the Gompa served as deterent to the attackers. The south and south-west side presents a steep climb. The main entrance to the Gompa is from North. The eastern side has a gradual slope and on this village - Sheyo. The water supply to the Gompa is from North. The source is at Lodrong near Brahmdungchong cave. The water, comes through underground drain, upto the main entrance of the Gompa at chikhang. (CHI- water, Khang - House). In the chikhang Dhunguer Mane (Water prayer wheel) keeps on rotating with the force of the water. The bell fixed in it produces Ting-Ting on every round. This water is considered sacred and free from cantamination.

Two paths from the right and left of chikhang meet at KaKaling. The Kakaling is constructed with stone and timber and is having a C.G.I. sheet roof. The Ceilings decorated with multi-coloured depiction of Mandala, the Mystic magic circles. The mandala is called "KiLkhor" and there are nine different mandalas depicting the nine supernatural Powers. The upper portion of the walls up to the ceiling were having many paintings of God, Goddesses and incarnated Lamas. In the front right hand wall was the blue painting of a fierce looking devine form "Ningme Chan" the ancient patron God of Tawang, riding a horse. This door canopy is called Kakaling and has its own importance. Every village has kakaling on both side of village. 'kah" means command and Ling means the area. To pass through the kakaling denotes that one has accepted the religious pass command of the area. To pay respect to the symbols and paintings of god, goddesses and lama, it is obligatory to remove ones head gear while entering the kakaling. The kakaling is situated at the narrowest part of the hillock which is about twenty feet. After the kakaling is the outer entrance of the Gompa which is always kept open.

The perimeter wall of the gompa starts from this outer entrance. The eastern perimeter up to the Southern entrance is 925ft. The height of the wall is ten ft. Above the outer entrance there are houses inhabited by the families of the employees of Gompa. After this outer entrance are some shops and BUMPA. There are two rooms in the BUMPA containing two chorten. The northern one having the statue of ChongKhapa the founder of Gelugpa sect and the other one of Lama Thangton GyalPo.

The inner entrance is after the BUMPA having heavy wooden doors and the entrance is closed at night. There is a school inside to the west of the path. The young boys entering the Lama hood are taught the three Rs as well as religious lessons in this school. The path goes from the back and left side of the Gompa. There is a specious courtyard in the front. All religious functions are held in this courtyard. To the north of this courtyard is the main Gompa, to the west the library, to the south the reserved grainary and main store and to the east the common kitchen of the Lamas.

Beneath the common kitchen are the sixty five small houses for the Lamas called "SHA". Residence of MERA LAMA was in the house situated to the east-south of the main Gompa. It is said that during the cremation of the body of Mera Lama, his tongue, heart and eyes did not burn to ashes. They became one mass. This mass along with the ashes are kept in a chorten in this house. The statue of MERA Lama is placed in the toran of the Chorten. The libarary called PARKHANG is in a three storeyed building to the west of the courtyard. It contains many manuscripts and also wood-block printed books. Two sets of 225 volume of Tangyur and three sets of 108 volumes of Kangyur, five sets of CHHANKIYA SUNG BUM, many rare editions of DORCHHOI, SUNG DUI and GYETONGPA in gold letters are kept here. On an altar in the libarary is the statue of CHONG KHAPA.

The main Gompa is to the north of the courtyard. This is three storied building and houses the assembly hall -DU-Khang, the temple and the labrang - the establishment of the KhenPo (Abbot). The assembly hall in the ground floor is 110 ft. by 80 ft. The walls of the large verandah through which one enters the Dukhang are decorated with colourful paintings. The wall - painting on the west of the main door is of the guardian Gods of southern direction LHOCHO GYALPO PHAGKYEPO and of eastern direction SHERCHO GYALPO THULKO SHUNG. Similarly on the eastern wall of the verandah is the painting of guardian God of western direction JHANG CHO GYALPO NAMTHESE. On the eastern wall of this verandah is the mural of SIBIKHROLO, the wheel of life depicting the six realms in which a person can be reborn. On the western wall is painting of the universe HRIRAP according to the Buddhist philosophy.

From this verandah the entrance is to the main hall. In this assembly hall there are two rows of 36 square huge wooden pillars at equal distance. Out of these, four pillars are very long and go up to support the ceiling of the first floor. The upper gallery of the first floor is supported by these 32 pillars. The hall gets sun light from a large sky-vent and six windows of the eastern wall. In the centre of the wall there are three CHUBRIS-open ended cylindrical cloth banners made of different colors of brocade hanging from the ceiling of the roof. During religious functions two rows of Lamas sit facing each other behind these between the wooden pillars. The height and placement of the seats are according to the seniority of the Lamas varying from one feet to four feet. The seats of senior Lamas are near the altar. From the north the first seat is of the KhenPo, the abbot. In front of him and slightly lower is the seat of 'LOPON' who initiates all ritual functions in the assembly hall and looks after the management of the monstery during the absence of Abbot. By his side the seat of UMDZE, the organizer of religious services, who leads the intoning of the hymns on such occasion. By the side of the seat of Khenpo is a lower seat for the visiting senior Lama. In the next row from the north there are three seats of equal height for THRIDA RIMPOCHE, SARONG RIMPOCHE and DOBLEY RIMPOCHE. Adjacent to the main entrance to the west there are two important seats, the higher one is of GERGO who maintains discipline in the assembly hall and also in the monastery. If any one desires to meet any senior Lama or if any Lama of the monastery wants to go out, they have to obtain permission of GERGO. By the side of GERGO'S seat, Slightly lower is the seat of CHUBRI, the assistant to GERGO.

In side of the Dukhang, colurful murals are made on the walls.

In the eastern wall is the painted image of SHOKPO JOMKHAR, on the southern wall NINGME CHAN and on the western wall eight medical Budhas called MANLHA DESHENGE and thirty five confessional Budhas in different MUDRAS called TUNGSHAKPA. Towards the eastern wall in the long wooden shelves are kept dancing costumes, ritual articles, wooden masks etc. Along the western wall towards the north are kept two chortens each of two feet height and a five feet statue of CHENREZI CHAGTONG CHANGTONG.

The altar of tutelary deity PALDEN LHAMU is approximately twelve feet high and 25 ft in length with the northern wall. To the left and right of this altar are the icons of different manifestations of Bodhistwa. It has two tiers. The statue of MERA LAMA and TANPIE DRONME are in the lower tier to the west. Above the wooden altar are two dragons carved in the wood. The altar has a silken curtain. Inside along with many precious small statues is kept in a silver casket the copper tube containing the silk cloth on which the 5th Dalai Lama has painted Palden Lhamu with his blood. The 5th Dalai Lama gave the sealed copper tube wrapped in a silk cloth. It is said that the copper tube is still retaining the warmth of the blood of 5th Dalai Lama. There fore people call it LHAMU JA- DOLMA. Mera Lama has kept it enclosed in a silver casket. Since then this has not been opened. Time to time senior Lamas can see the casket inside the altar after some specified religious ceremony.

To the east of this altar are established CHONGKHAPA and crowned Budha statue with his two disciples MODGALYAN and SARIPUTRA. To the east of these statue is the small golden image of white Tara "DUKAR CHAGTONG CHANGTONG UTONG. Adjacent to it the seat of the present fourteen Dalai Lama which he occupied on coming to India for the first time in 1959. The door to the inner sanctum is by the side of this seat. To the east of this door is another wooden shelf 20 ft in length and approximately 12 ft in height. It contains a number of statues of God, Goddesses and incarnated Lamas. The first statue is of sixth Dalai Lama Lobang Changyang Gyatso a MONPA born in Tawnag in the year 1683.

The inner hall Chhan- Khang is about sixty feet by twenty feet. On entering the hall, along the southern wall there are eight images in standing posture of eight different menifestation of Budha. These are Awalokiteshwar (Chen - Reji) Maitreye (JAMPA) Akhsyagarbha (Kunto -JANG-PO), VajraPani (Chana Dorjee), Manjushree (JamPe-yang) Sarva Nivaran Vishkambhini (DriPa Thamje Nampar Selva) and Kshitigarbha (Sve Ningpo). Collectively they are called Nipe She Chinge. Next these are six images of fearsome deities, the defenders of Buddhist religion against the demons and other enemies. These are Jigje, GonPo, Chhoige, Palden Lhamu, Namshe and Chamsing. These ferocious images are kept behind a curtain.

In the centre of Chhan - Khang there is a 27 ft high statue of Budha in Padamsan on a platform, called Stonba Sakya Thuba. Along the northern wall, to the east of this statue there is a five feet high stupa containing the ashes of Thechpa Rimpoche. This Stup is called Kudung. ThechPa Rimpoche was the founder of sub-sect Tarsar of Ningma sect and was from Mindolin Gompa in Tibbet. The present incarnation of Thechpa Rimpoche, Lama Urgen lives in Khinme Gompa below Tawnag. Next to it is another stupa six feet high Dungten of the mother of the sixth Dalai Lama and Kudung of Lama TanPie Dromne. From this inner hall wooden steps lead to the upper storey. On climbing to this chamber there is an impressive image of Guru Padamshambhawa situated to the north-east. To the west of this are kept a few small icons and copper chortens. Next to these are the images of the Tibbetan Regent of the time of the 5th and 6th Dalai Lama.

On the western part of the northern wall and the western wall are thirty five images of Budha of confession in wooden case. On the southern wall are the paintings of twenty renowned Pandits. Among these five are Indian Pandits Lalitvajra, Amoghavajra, Padmavajra, Ishijungme and Atish

Dipankar. The remaining fifteen are of Tibbetan scholars-Ralhochowa, DorgeeDak, Ra Yeshi Senge, Rache Rop, Ra Bumshen, Je Jongalo. RongPa Sherap, Lama Eshi, Choi Che Dondrum Rinchin, Panchen Choige Gechhan, Drupechin Choi Dorjee, Gyalwa Loshan Dondrum, Khechup Sange Eshi, Jechun Lobsang Choigen, Kesang Khetup, and Nawang Chutum Domden.

There are number of rooms on the first floor. The largest room is called Chhang Khang Che, having four huge square wooden Pillars. Next room is called Lo-Ling having seven such Pillars. In this room is an artistically made, colourful replica of a palace signifying imaginary heaven. The Palace is called Jigjeloi Lang the Palace of tutelary God of Gelugpas - Jigje - Vajra Bhairav. The palace holds inside an image of Jigje in close embrace with his consort Yum Dorjee Drolma. Remaining rooms are the residence, meeting room, kitchen etc of the abbot- Khen Po.

The upper most storey is empty. This is used as visitors gallery during the ceremonies especially during Torgey. The imposing building of the monastery is very impressive.

The founder of this Gompa Lama Lodro Gyatso popularly known as Mera Lama was the first propagator of Budhism in MonPa area. He was the fourth incarnation of Lama TanPie Dronme. The second incarnation of Lama Tanpie Dronme was Lama Lobsang TanPie. The third incarnation Lama Lobsang TanPie Gechen was born in Tsona Mondop village in Tibbet and the fifth incarnation Lama Lobsang Tapgeya was born in Kham region of Tibet. He traveled to Bhutan and Bodh Gaya, came to Tawang and got constructed the assembly hall DU- Khang of the GomPa. He died in Tawang. The sixth incarnation Lama kejang Doyen Tabjing was also born in Tibet. He got his education in SERA monastery and on completion of his education came to Tawang. He visited Dirang, Lish Phudung and sherkudpen area. He got constructed Kharsadung Gompa of Dirang and a Gompa at Rupa during the year 1742. He initiated the villagers of Lish in to Budhism and prohibited animal sacrifice and freed them from the old belief. He went back to his native place Ehlagiri in Tibet and expired there. The seventh incarnation Lama Kejang Guerme was also born at Ehlagiri in Tibet. He completed his education in SERA monastery and came to Tawang. He traveled to Bodh Gaya and Sanchi. While returning to Tawang he expired at Dirang. The eighth incarnation Thubten kejang was born in Lhobrak region of Tibet. On completion of his education he stayed in Tapko Drachang monastery of Tibet. After that he came to Tawang and spent his time in Tashi Tsoling Gompa at Sakteng, Bhutan and Tawang Gompa. He was popularly known as Guru Rimpoche. After 1962 he came to stay at Bomdila and later expired here.

Ninth and present incarnation Lama Tenzing Thrinle Namo is born at Rama Camp, 5 Kms from Dirang on Tawang road, in 1967 in the house of Ningma Lama Rapten. After his birth his mother Pema Chhodron was mentally deranged for some years. According to his father Lama Rapten the child when he was three years old, used to take one or two of his clothess and walk out from the house. When asked, his reply was that he is going his home. On further enquiry about his home he used to indicate his finger towards Tawang and Sakteng in Bhutan During this period the metarnal uncle of the child, himself a lama came to his house from Vill. Khrimu. The eighth incarnation had given a bowl to him. When in the morning the lama, maternal uncle of the child used to perform religious rituals with the bowl, the child used to come to him and point to the bowl saying that this belongs to him.

After observing these utterings and actions of the child, it was reported to Rigya Rimpoche of Tawang Monastery. Taking into account the date, time and place of the birth of this child, the learned Lamas of Tawang monastery came to the conclusion that the child may be the ninth incarnation of Lama TanPie Dronme. The parents have named the child Pema Tanzin but Rigya Rimpoche Changed the name to Thuptan Choizor.

The complete story was sent to Dalai Lama at Dharamshala. On instructions of Dalai Lama the child prodigy was taken to Tawang monastery. On a fixed auspicious date the ritual of final determination of the incarnation commenced at Tawang Gompa. Two slips of paper with the writings "Incarnation" and "No Incarnation" were sealed in two small balls of flour of the same weight and size. These were kept in a bowl and a lama stood under the altar of Palden Lhamu with the bowl in hand. With incantation of mantra the lama started swaying to and fro the bowl infront of the altar. In this process one of the flour balls fell out from the bowl. The remaining ball when opened was found to have containing the slip of paper with the writing INCARNATION. This process was repeated two more times and every time the ball containing the slip 'incarnation' was retained in the bowl. Some more tests were carried out in which the child recognized and picked up the tea-cup and other items of personal use of late Guru Rimpoche out of the lot of similar looking items. After that he was confirmed as Incarnation of Guru Rimpoche Mera Lama and was sent to Dharamshala for education and training in Lamaism, under the supervision of Dalai Lama. Initially he was permitted to visit Dirang -Tawang once in two to three years. But now he comes to Dirang and Tawnag every year. On completion of his education and training he will be established as abbot

(KhenPo) of Tawang Monastery. At present the duties and responsibilities of abbot is performed by a senior Lama appointed by the Dalai Lama.

The incarnated Lamas are called "Yangshipa" or "Rimpoche". There is no such Incarnation in SherdukPen area. In MonPa area the line of two of Incarnations of Lamas of Ningma sect and eleven incarnated lamas of Gelugpa sect are continuing. Among these all are not important. There were a few such personalities who made an everlasting impression on the psyche of laity of their spiritual achievements. Guru RimPoche is one of such Incarnation.

The Dalai Lama is the Incarnated reflex from the celestial Bodhisttwa-Avalokiteshwar, while the other Incarnated Lamas of this area are re-born Lamas and saints. The child in which such a Bodhisattwa is reborn retains the knowledge of previous life.

Tawang has the honor of being the birth place of the sixth Dalai Lama. The Sixth Dalai Lama Lobsang Rinchin Chhangeye Gyatso was born here on 1st march 1683. His parents Lama Rinchin Tashi a Ningma Lama and mother Chhowang Lhamu were residing in Urgeyeling Gompa where he was born.

Urgeyeling Gompa is one of the Gompa of Ningma sect called Lingsum. The story of his birth also has a devine touch. It is said that prior to his birth his mother Chhewang Lhamu had gone to the stream below the eastern side of the Gompa where she found a Golden "Dorjee" in the stream. She picked it up and put it inside her garment touching her stomach. When she came to the house with the water container she found that the object has vanished. After this incident she gave birth to a handsome healthy child.

During that period the political situation in Tibet was such that the news of the death of the fifth Dalai Lama was kept a secret for fourteen years by the regent Deshi Sange Gyatso. In these fourteen years this MonPa lad had developed in to a happy go lucky person in the healthy and lush green atmosphere of Tawang and open MonPa society. But he possessed the sharp intellect and wisdom being the reflex from celestial Bodhisattwa.

The lack of proper education and training had turned him in to an unsophisticated care free young boy. He revel with his friends in practicing archery, drinking Chhang, composing songs and singing them in his modulated voice, showing unique skill in "CHHAM" dance and roaming in the beautiful glades of Tawang.

When a group of Lamas in disguise came to Tawang to Urgeling Gompa in search of this Incarnated boy he was playing at a short distance in the forest. His mother called his name and he could know that the Lamas had come to take him away. He wrote on a rock with his finger "Lama Kheno""God. Please". He had perhaps some inclination of his future days and he had invoked and submitted himself to God.

He was taken to Lhasa. In the month of September year 1697 he was made to take the vow of "Getsul Dompa". In the same year he was put on the Golden throne in Lhasa's Potala palace and was made the temporal head of Tibet. But this life of discipline, restrictions, solitude and sadness was unacceptable to the youthful mind of this Monpa lad which revolted against this strict regimen, and instead of progressing further from the status of Getsul to Gelong Lama he even renounced his Getsul Dompa status and shunned the lama habit. In the palace he started brewing his own tea and serving it to guests. With occasional night of revelary laced with Chhang, song and dance in the company of friends. His archery sessions continued. His poetical compostions are very akin to the couplets of Kabir in their devine connotation. Because of his melodious songs and voice he was also known as the limitless (infinite) ocean of sweet melodies. His rise in fame was more on account of his romantic sentimental poems and gifted voice. Despite his continued disinterest to the Lamaist order of life the people of Tibet and the followers of Budhism loved him. He gave a new form, meaning and dimension to the dance and dance forms of Tibet. Even today his compositions are sung by the older generation in Tawang and Pangchen areas. Many of the words in his songs have lost their original meanings or have been distorted over the years and it is with great difficulty that one can decipher their meanings. Compilation of his songs in the pangchen area was difficult and laborious. It is to a very limited extent that the meanings and notions conveyed in his songs have been brought out in the trasanlations. The translation of some of the songs sung by the villagers in Pangchen area are:-

i. Her sweet smile flashed on the drinking crowd but her eyes expressed her love to me only.

ii. With the bar- maid and plenty of wine one remains fearless and in heaven.

iii. If my beloved who has stolen my heart, renounces the world for the sake of religion then my youth will search a shelter in some hermitage.

As the story of the birth of Dalai Lama Changyang Gyatso is full of miracles and mysteries so is his life. He showed some miracles at Urgeling Gompa during his childhood. It is stated that while leaving Urgeling he planted his stick near Gompa which grew into three sandal wood trees. He had said that when all the three trees will come to the same size and height he will come to Tawang. In 1959 the people of Tawang saw that the three trees have come to the same size and height. But they were astounded to see one day fire flames emanating from these trees. Just after this incident the fourteenth Dalai Lama came to Tawang from Tibet.

The belief is very common and strong among the populace that the 6th Dalai Lama took birth in Tawang to fulfill his promise made to Mera Lama as he couldnot come to Tawang that time.

According to a myth the regent Deshi Sange Gyatso had requested to 5th Dalai Lama that the succession to the position of the Dalai Lama should be made hereditary so that on every occasion the time and money invested in searching, locating, educating and training of a new incarnation are saved.

Further till the Dalai Lama attains the adulthood, the responsibility of his post is carried by the regent. The 5th Dalai Lama had said that his next incarnation may be allowed to take a recourse to this unhindered. It is believed that if the sixth Dalai Lama had been allowed to meet and marry his beloved, this position of Dalai lama would have been hereditary and Tibet a powerful state. One of the songs of changyang Gyatso expresses this

i. If I would have married my beloved. I would have been happy as if I have found all the precious gems form the sea bed.

ii. The swan desires to stay in the lake out of his love but the snow is covering the water of the lake and the swan flies off without repentance.

The regent deshi Sange Gyatso, undermining the instruction of the 5th Dalai Lama tried to put Changyang Gyatso under the strict regimen of Lamaism, but the young Chhangyang Gyatso revolted against this strict discipline. Some people when came to know about his conduct raised a doubt whether he is the true incarnation of Dalai Lama or not. This was solved by a renowned astrologer and soothsayer who declared him as the true incarnation of 5th Dalai Lama and this enhanced the respect, reverence and faith of the populace.

The political turmoil of Tibet further made the sixth DalaiLama dejected. In 1700, Lhazang Khan of Magnolia removed the sixth Dalai Lama from his post, imprisoned him and took him with them. On the way at Gounganor during the month of November 1700, the sixth Dalai Lama vanished from the captivity of Mongol army. The mongol soldiers spread the news of his demise. The people blamed the mongol army of his assassination. Amidst this mystery it is said that the sixth Dalai Lama was appearing in central Tibet, Mongolia, India and Nepal and had conducted religious rites at several places. The general belief is that he left this world in the year 1746.

The seventh Dalai Lama was born at Lithang. This was indicated in one of the songs of sixth Dalai Lama.

White cranes! Lend me your wings. I won't go very far, I will return from Lithang.

Tawang Monastery

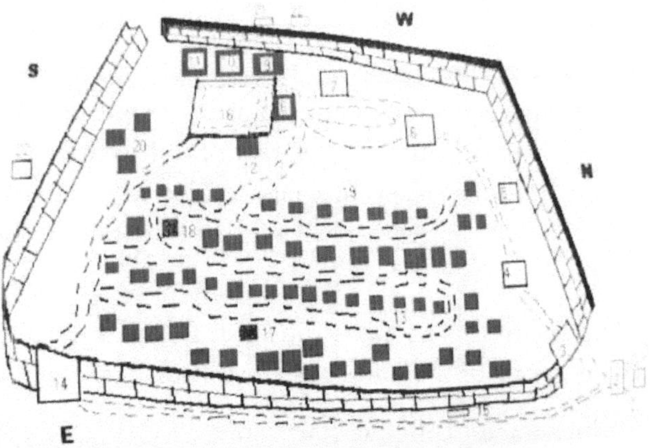

Layout of Tawang Monastery and legend of the layout

Legend – Tawang Monastery

1. Chikhang	Water House
2. Kakaling	Door Canopy
3. Gyasko Chhema	Outer Entrance
4. Chhong Khang	Shops
5. Bumpa	Rooms Containing Chorfen
6. Gyasko Nangma	Inner Entrance
7. Lapta Khang	School
8. DU Khang	Main Gompa
9. Par Khang	Library
10. Chhan Khang	Reserve Store
11. Booh	Main Store
12. Rum Khang	Kitchen
13. Hostel	
14. Lhou Gasko	Southern Entrance
15. Doko Mane	Mane Wall
16. Douje	Court Yard
17. Dilapidated Houses	The colony of 65 houses inhabited by Lamas
18. Sha	Residnece of Lamas
19. The Residence of Mera Lama	
20. Toilets	
21. Latrines	

MONYUL

	Indian Name	Tibetan Name
1.	Nagarjun	Palgon Lutup
2.	Naro	Dupchen Naropa
3.	Swet Tara	Dolma Karpo Lhamu
4.	Harit Tara	Dolma Changshiru Lhamu
5.	Sant Rakshit	Palden Jiwachho
6.	Atish Dipankar	Jowo Chhinpo And Palden Atisha
7.	Gyalwa Rimpoche	First Dalai Lama
8.	Vajra Dhara	Dorjee Chan
9.	Marpa	Jetsun Marpa
10.	Marich/Varah	Ojer Changma
11.	Amitabh	Chhe Pame
12.	Kuber	Jam Balha
13.	Awalokiteshwar	Chen Rejig
14.	Vajra Varahi	Dorjee Fakmo
15.	Amit-Ayu	Oyi Pame
16.	Manjushree	Jampeyang

CHAPTER SEVEN

Dakpa Chhogeyat

The region west of Tawang is comparatively more green and populated. Dakpachhogeyat means the eight regions. This starts from west of Tawang towards Lumla after crossing Kangten bridge from kidung meadow. This region is out of Chhoksum. The region starts form kidung meadow and includes Shakyur, Sakpret, Thongleng. Lumla, Kharung. Shakti, and across Namjang Chu Muktur and Khoblitang villages. The villages of Shakti, Muktur and khoblitang are also separtately called Mokhasak sum. Ginger, garlic and chillies are mainly cultivated in this area. Now there is a road between Tawang to Lumla. Prior to construction of the road the 35 kms bridal path was there and the first staging hut was at village Thongleng.

Thongleng produces maximum harvest of Ginger and garlic. After Lumla the bridal path goes to Pangchen area via villages Ghispu and Shakti. Exotic orchids, rhodendron red flowers, white lily and different colours of wild flowers are found in abundance by the side of the bridal path from Tawang to Lumla and Lumla to Pangchen.

In 1966 we marched from Tawang and reached Thongleng via villages Pamghar and Sakpret. The night was spent in the staging hut made of logs and bamboo. Second day we reached Lumla. Third day we reached vill. Shakti via

Yarbang, Sherbang, and Ghispu. while leaving Lumla, one Monpa friend and well- wisher cautioned me not to accept any eatable in the villages from unknown persons. Even not to take the Pack - Lunch in presence of any villager. When I insisted to know the reason, he explained that in these villages there is an old practice to administer poison in food which is based on their age old superstition. In these villages there are some people who suffer from the superstition that if they administer poison in the food or drink of a person and the person dies, his good fortune will be inherited by the person who administer poison. Therefore they administer white powder of Aconite root in the food or drink. This Aconite root Powder is a slow poison. It affects the liver and the person dies in due course.

Aconite plants are found in plenty at the high altitude meadows. During the months of August September their dark violate colour flowers adorn the lush green meadows. After the month of October the plant wilts. The villagers take out the roots from under the wilted plants and dry it in shade. The dried roots are used as medicine. Small dose of aconite powder is given to the cattles affected with cold. Very small dose is also mixed in 'Chhang' to make it strong; The local name of aconite root is "Chandok". The extensive belief in "Mantra- Tantra" of the populace in this area even led them to believe that evil eyes can also poison the food. But observing the liberal hospitality of the Monpas it was difficult for me to believe these stories. Inspite of the cautions given to me by my well wishers, I accepted the hospitality, the food and drinks offered to me in each of these villages.

Many occasions came when I had to stay in village-Shakti. In the evening a number of villagers used to assemble at the staging hut and narrate local folk tales. The eighty years old blind man Seng Gombu narrated the story related to the establishment of this village - Shakti.

Village Shakti is divided into two parts. The upper part consisting of twenty five houses is called Rangaten. The lower part of twelve houses is called Wormang. Besides these few hamlets have come up with the new -cultivations below and above Wormang. These are named Kraiteng. Changklan and Tadung. The boundary of Shakti Village starts from the large stream after village GhisPu. Before reaching Kakling of Shakti there is a small hamlet called Neyermang or "Neela Idung". The boundary of vill Shakti in the north is Khepabra, in the west Namjang Chu and Choktur La in the east. Across Choktur La is the sacred Lake of this area ThangaPhe Tso.

According to Meme Seng Gombu, once upon a time four men Bili Pabjee and their four sons Bili Bupjee came from the country of Lord Budha to TribLa via Durang and Selaghar in Bhutan.

They were fearless hunters and were in look out for new places. From TribLa they saw this area and assessed that this is a suitable area for hunting as well as for habitation. They came here after crossing the river Namjang Chu and constructed a dwelling at Neyermang. The oldest son also constructed a Gompa and wanted to establish the statue of "Chhoisung Guru DakPa" But due to some unknown reason he could not do so and now that Gompa is also no more there.

They discovered that the water from the stream Lishku fobJang, which originates from the hill Brahshache beneath choktur La is very healthy and good to drink. They decided to inhabit the plain area below this stream. After some time, one day when these four youngmen were going on their hunting trip to Taksang Gompa along a stream they found on the sands of the stream small foot prints of a woman. Amazed and full of curiosity the four youngmen sat in the forest there hidden in bushes. In the evening they saw a young girl coming from Taksang Gompa side. With their bow and arrow these four young men surrounded the girl. The young girl said that she is not a wild animal but the forest -Goddess. And they should not harm her. The brothers brought her with them to their dwelling and married her. Out of this wedlock with the "Van -Kanya" for many years they got a son and a daughter alternately and they established this village- Shakti. The clans residing above Shakti village are called "solayee jom" and those residing below are "BrokPajom". After some more years one of the brothers named "PonBhalu" found a book (Pecha) in a stream Kerchhi in Serthi Greng north of the village near "Pholi-Phu". Ponbhalu was literate. He read the book and taught the people Broh dance and songs. At the same place he also found a monkey-Mask. (PRA- BA). In the Broh dance males only take part. One of them put on the monkey-mask and the remaining six male dancers remain without mask.

The whole village is of GelugPa sect. In the village Gompa there is the statue of "Sange Jamba Gombu". The Gompa has hand-written sixteen volumes of "BUM" and one volume of "Sherbum". They pay voluntary contribution to Tawnag Gompa called "Khreey". After the New Year Losar, the lama from Tawang monastery comes here to collect "Khreey". Khoblitang villagers across Namjang Chu also pay Khreey to Tawang monastery. They send load of grains to Shakti. The villagers of Shakti take these loads of grains and other items to vill-Ghispu. From there the contributions collected in kinds are taken from one village to another and reaches Tawang monastery. From ancient time this system of religious contribution from these villages to Tawnag Gompa is continuing smoothly.

After village Shakti the area called Pangchen starts. The bridal path form Shakti goes through fields, streams and decends at Namjang Chu at khepa Bra. At khepaBra there is a steel wire rope bridge with bamboo mattings. After crossing the bridge the path goes along the river. A small hamlet above kharekPo called Thokeling is of five - six houses. They are immigrants from Bhutan. This area belongs to village - Muchut of Pangchen.

Pangchen means a vast sprawling meadow. Generally all the inhabitants of the region are called monpa but the people of Pangchen maintained a separate identity of themselves. They do not call themselves monpa but BEMI which means a superior or exalted race having devine protection and blessings. The six months stay at zimithang provided me ample opportunity to become familiar with the people of Lumpu, Sokchen, Muchut, kharmin and kelengteng. These five villages are called DING DUK the six Ding. Ding denots the ancient electoral area. Sokchen village has three Ding .Tyon Ding (Upper Ding) Pai Ding (middle Ding) Me Ding (lower Ding), Village Lumpu, Karmin and Kelengteng one Ding each.

According to the old man meme Tsering Sonam of Vill- Lumpu and Sri Kesang of vill - Muchut, Pangchen was a hidden place in the lap of Nature. Its four entrances on four directions were guarded by local deities and Tantalus (Asur). The southern entrance while coming from Shakti is at PholiPhu or Phor Phu. There is a cave here and after it a bridge which has been constructed by putting logs in the holes made in the steep rock wall. The entrance is said to be guarded by Asurs called "GonPo".

The eastern entrance is on the path coming from Tawang via Sungetsher at a distance of three Kms. before reaching

Taksang Gompa. There was a huge rock with some carvings on it which has been destroyed in the process of road construction. The Northern entrance is on the path coming from Khinjemane before reaching Drokam Samba Bridge. By the side of the river Namjangchu in the forest is a sangphum and near it a two and half feet stone pillar embedded in the ground. This stone pillar looks like a humane figure and called KUNG KUKPA. The previous bridge on Namjang Chu was at this place. Kung means corner stone, KukPa means an embecile. The folk-lore states that the soul of an embecile is in this stone and it guards the Northern entrance.

The western entrance is at the cave Pilanas at Sirkim. The villagers come to this place on auspicious days for worshipping and putting coloured prayer flags.

This unknown region during ancient time was very prosperous. There were more than hundred houses. To prove this the villagers showed us ruins of about fifteen houses in the forest above village Muchut. The Dukpas from Bhutan had raided these villages.

The raiders had come from Bhutan via Manam La above village Lumpu and from south crossing Trib La via villages Muktur and Khoblitang. The inhabitants of Pangchen fought them with their bow and arrows and long swords and defeated and drove away the DukPas. From the south the raiders had come up to the stream coming out from Bludi Tso. A fierce battle took place at this stream. During this battle the people of Pangchen cut and removed the five downward pointing ends of their cap "Kanglumjamo" because the warriors found them hindering their sight. Now while the Monpas of Dirang and Tawnag still have these five downward pointing ends in their yak hair cap, the Pangchen people wear a simple round cap of yak hair, called "MaujemyanPa" or "Uyi". Around it they put a band of peacock feather. The cap looks like a helmet. Another type of cap is also worn called. "Sirja". This is wollen cap with a four inches round band of woven woolen material of orange, mauve and blue colour. This type of cap was made popular by Ningma Lamas.

The Budhist Lamaism was propogated here by lamas from Tibet. According to a folk tale a lama came to their area via Chamling La and propogated Ningma sect. After this their interactrion with Tibet started. Mera Lama came to Pangchen after construction of Tawang Gompa. On the way MeraLama took rest at a cave Pemang Phu. There he observed a stone moving on its own and the stone followed him when he resumed his journey on foot. Mera Lama took the stone and brought it to Pangchen. He told to the villagers about this stone. Impressed with this amazing stone, the villagers offered to pay every year yak butter equal to the weight of the stone from each milch yak. The offering of yak butter to Tawnag Gompa is still continuing and this system is called "MARTHE". The stone is preserved at Tawnag Monastery. Every year a Lama from Tawnag monastery comes to this area with the stone to collect Marthe. With the influence of Mera Lama GelugPa sect flourished in the area. The influence of both the sects NingmaPa and GelugPa can be seen in this area.

The bridal Path after crossing Khepabra Bridge was earlier passing through Pemang Phu. But due to the erosion caused by Namjang Chu, now the path goes over and behind the cave. During rains the cave is full of Namjang Chu water. The cave is not providing shelter to passers by.

After a few years of the construction of Tawang Gompa a Ningma Lama came to Pangchen from Jhanu region of Tibet and stayed in village Kharmin. Here he begot a son from a village woman named MandeJomba. In Monpa society the child born out of wedlock is called JAOU and gets proper place in the society. One day when Mandejomba kept the child in a bamboo basket by the side of the field where she was working, a huge monkey came and took away the child on a tree. After invoking the dieties and making some offering the monkey brought back and kept the child in the basket. After this incident the child was called PRADAR. (PRA - Monkey, DAR -given). The child went to Tibet and returned after achieving full Lama hood. He was known as Lama Pradar.

On returning from Tibet one night he got a dream to make a stupa in this area. He expressed his desire to the villagers. All the five villages wanted that the stupa should be constructed in their village. To sort out this problem, Lama Pradar sat in meditation and invited celestial direction. He got it in his dream that the stupa should be constructed at the site near Gorsam (Gor- Rock. SAM- Bridge). Now to decide the shape and size of the stupa, he went to Kathmandu with some of his friends and brought the design of Bodhinath Stupa cut on a thick radish. When he came back the radish has dried and shrunk therefore the size of Gorsam Chorten is smaller than Bodhinath stupa. At this place there was a stone bridge over Namjang Chu.

After this the design made on the radish was taken to Bhutan and DURANG Chorten was constructed there. As the radish has further shriveled the size of Durang Chorten became smaller than Gorsam chorten.

The base of Gorsam Chorten is 168 ft by 168 ft and the perimeter of its dome is of approximately 220 ft and height 215 ft. On the 168'X168' stone platform there is another square platform 8ft wide and 160'X160'. Like this there are five square platforms one over another. Above this is the dome which is the sanctum. Inside the sanctum are kept three sets each of 108 copper icons of Budha and three sets of 108 copper miniature of the chorten. The dome sanctum is crowned by a square capitol TORAN. Above the Toran is pyramidal spire. Chooramani of thirteen steps like segments, depicting the thirteen Bodhisattwa heavens. In North-east direction there is a door in the dome. Inside there are two levels in the dome. There are eight steps from the lower level to upper level. In April 1987 the four wooden pillars inside the lower level were replaced by the stone pillars as they had become very old and decayed. The upper level still have the six wooden pillars. Inside, the height of central pole is about forty feet. It took fourteen years to complete the construction of this chorten. The size of stones used in the construction are 10'X3'X1'. These stones have round holes at one end as they were brought here from distant hills by pulling with ropes tied in the hole.

The oldest village in Pangchen is Lumpu. The old community hall is still existing. From olden days the system of assembling the people of remaining four villages by giving smoke signal is still invogue. The clan at Lumpu village is Shengmo. The villager of Khoblitang are also shengmo. They have settled there migrating from LumPu. The Lamas of the four villages are from Shunmo clan. The other clans are Gyamo, Nhamo and Shromo The clan born from wedlock between Tibetan and Monpas are Khumo. Pangchen people as yet have no marriage relations with Bhutan.

During my six months stay at Zimithang I developed rapport with the people of all the five villages. I also learn the good lauguage to some extent, and noticed that the accent and style of speech differs from village to village. While the people of Sokchen and to some extent of Lumpu and Muchut speak in soft tone stretching the words, the tone and style of Kharmin and kelengteng is harsh and fast.

All the social, religious and administrative busincses of these villages are conducted in a democratic way. For administration they select their village headman called "Chorgen". For religious and social activities and solving the internal matters they select another head man called KANCHEN. In Lumpu village every year during the month of November the selection of KANCHEN is held. The milieu of this selection is very interesting.

The present Kanchen stands in front of the assembly with a pot of Chhang and appeals to the assembly that his one year term as Kanchen has come to its end and he should be now freed from the responsibility of this appointment. He also proposes the name for the new Kanchen and begs to be forgiven for his mistakes during this tanure of one year. The name for the new kanchen is always decided informally among the villagers. The person whose name is now formally proposed stands up and strongly objects to his nomination stating that he has neither desire nor the ability to shoulder the responsibility of this post. But he is pressurized by the assembly and every one offers him a cup of Chhang. In this way in an atmosphere of bonhomie and exchange of free flowing Chhang the new Kanchen is selected. Prior to Budhism, Bon religious practices were prevalent in Pangchen and local deities were being worshipped. Now only one or two Bonpu Lamas are here and that too in village Sokchen only. They perform "Lhase" religious ceremony once in a year. The local worshipping rites which have been accepted in Budhism are Kongo Punsum and Gompa Punsum. KongoPonsum is performed at the isolated hill feature situated north west of village Lumpu at a distance of one days march. This mountain peak from a distance look like a human form wearing a hat.

Below this peak is a lake spread in two acres, and by the side of the lake is a cave in which six to seven persons can stay. After thawing of snow during summer the villagers come to this place and put coloured prayer flags.

Gompa Punsum is towards Hatung La. There are three peaks in a row and behind these is a large lake. These three peaks are called three brothers. From June to October every year the villagers come to this place. The track up to this place is difficult and beyond every one's to negotiate the terrain. Physically fit persons who can come to this place are requested to carry the offerings of coloured flags by those who are unable to take this arduous journey. On this route is another hill feature is called "MAKPON DAMPA" which is considered as the commander-in-chief of the diety. Here several rocks resemble like soldiers laced with different weapons.

In the high reaches above pangchen are two scenic places 'Bludi Tso' and 'kemela Tso. Nestled amidst the meadows at an attitude of 14000' the two lakes present a heavenly spectacle. In the latter half of Aug' 72 along with our colleagues Shri Pema Wangchuk, Shri Kesang of vill Muchut and a few villagers of Pangchen we set off for Bludi Tso Via Kharekpo. Crossing Pegrek we set up camp at ChiBrock below MarkangLa for a night. The next day we reached Bludi Tso after a steep climb. The lake formed from a glacier reflected the clear azure sky. Huge yaks were grazing in the beautiful meadows. The clanging of their bells the only sound breaking the loud silence of the place. Blue popies and violet aconite flowers dotted the landscape. For shelter the graziers (Brokpa) had walled the mouth of a cave with rocks leaving a narrow opening. The interior was quite comfortable with a carpet of dry grass covering the hard rocky surface. We stayed for two nights at this place. By evening SSB jawan kulanand sharma had served us tea and coffee. The night was starry and moonlit and ignoring the cold we sat out till late, in the night. Thinle aka "Bhalu" in a smattering of monpa and hindi regaled us with his tales of Ghosts, fairies and the supernatural beings who visit the place. The entire ambience was having a profound spell binding effect on the members of the group - Chimmi, Ananta Acharya and Tenzing. We finally got into our sleeping bags but due to the altitude or because of our experiences of the previous day we woke up early. Kulanand Sharma came with customery greeting of 'Jai Hind' and mug of tea. The day was bright and clear but we feared dense fog in the afternoon. We set off early for kemala Tso, 2 Kms. away from Bludi Tso. Kemela Tso did not disappoint us. It was equally beautiful as Bludi Tso. The clear water of the lake reflecting the green granite rock face of a cliff overlooking it. After scouring the area in and around Kemala Tso we returned back to our shelter at Bludi Tso coming across a flock of colourful pheasants and Monal on the way back. As anticipated a dense shroud of fog enveloped the area in the afternoon.

Bewitched by the amazing sights and filled with the marvelous joys of sky high peaks and mountain ridge we decided to trek along the watershed boundary between India & Bhutan upto Bleating. Starting well before sunrise we reached khaktangLa 15000'. In the afternoon crossing Lumpula & Markangla both at 14000'. True to its name the climb upto khaktangLa was along a torturous winding path full of sliding falling stones. At one place we were treated to a sight of a musk deer at a watering hole some 300' below us. Surprisily it continued to gaze curiously at us with no fear, till we were out of sight. A sudden heavy downpour in the afternoon made us scurry for shelter in the rhodendron bushes with our rain coats on. Thoroughly drenched we prepared tea in the evening after the rain ceased. There was gruel of 'sattu' mixed in the tea. We retired for the night in our wet cloths, wet sleeping bags and on a soaking wet earth.

The morning downed bright and sunny. Standing on the mountain ridge the Lumla region unfolded to our east while to the west was the Tashi yangshe Dzong in Bhutan. JongpingLa, MirguLa, TribLa, BrohongLa and JongfuLa (12723) were negotiated before we reached Bletting on the sixth day. Our expedition, had started from an attitude of 6000' and after traversing heights of 15000 ft culminated again at 6000 ft. Bludi Tso and KemeLa Tso are considered sacred places. We were cautioned against washing our socks, hankerchiefs and dirty utensils in the lake. We drew water from these lakes and washed at a distance.

Pangchen i.e.zimithang valley was a beautiful fertile valley before being ravaged by flood. A large part of Lumpu village was spread on the banks of the Namjangchu. The erstwhile Chorgen Narwangdi had a large sprawling house in this lower Lumpu. Kesang along with his family also used to reside here. Both banks of the River used to yield good crops. We used to take a strole in the evenings from Brokenthang to the other end of the valley. Invariably a religious or social ceremony would be taking place in the houses of the valley and we would be invited to attend. In addition to the chhang & Ara served as customary hospitality there would be a special delicacy - chhemin a paste of yak milkcheese and hot red chillies with salt. Alongwith it there would also be a halwa of either millet, maize or barley sattu boiled in water called 'JAN'. Unprocessed cheese churpi is kept in closed leather pouches. It not only turns bluish black in colour but also emits an unbearable smell. It is particularly repulsive to those not accustomed to it. This emboldened my friend Mr. Wangchuk to challenge me "your experiences of pangchen would be incomplete if you have not savoured the taste of Churpi", he remarked. We were in Sokchen in the house of the late Chorgen Dropen. Dinner was ready. Taking up the challenge I took recourse to Ara. The effect numbed my olefactory senses and helped me in slowly eating the churpi.

Somewhat similar was our experience of Aconite poisoning. We had been invited to Narwangdi's place. Two big Wooden casks of chhang had been placed. A man was playing the string instrument 'Damiang' and singing songs of the sixth Dalai Lama. The festivities started at eleven in the morning. Snacks were served with the Chhang. Several rounds of chhang had been Consumed by evening and continued into the night. Our lips and tongue became numb. Mr. Wangchu sitting besides me and some others felt their facial muscles being stretched. Suddenly Mr. Wangchuk said "Lets go - they have laced the chang with chandok". We manged to reach kesang's house and were made to vomit and drink a small glass of warm Ara. By morning I had recovered but many others were beset with loose motions for months. On being confronted, Narwangdi sheepishly admitted to having used the chandok to make the chhang strong. A few years later Narwangdi and his daughter Peki died of aconite poisoning.

When in a hurry to reach Tawang, we would take the route above Kharmin and after spending the night in Taksang Gompa reach Tawang the next day crossing GamraLa enroute. If not pressed for time we would spend the night in Serthang Gompa above Sokchen village. The next day after crossing Chamlingla, I would halt with Brokpas in the meadows of Grolithang. Atop the ChamingLa was akin to being on the roof of world. To the west one could see Sumdo, HathungLa and the Namka Chu valley while to the south the village of Ghispu was visible. Just below ChamlingLa is Chamling Tso which even on clear days is coverd in a layer of clouds. As per folk lore fairies come here to bathe. On descending further there is another small lake. Innumerable BrahmaKamal dot the rock face bordering this lake in the month of September. On the third day we would reach Taksang Gompa and on the fourth Tawang via Sungatser and GamraLa. During these treks there would be no hurry to reach our destination. The lure of grazing ground, hospitality of our Brokpas, the taste of Chhemin and Jan as well as the fascinating folk tales would be the main aim. I was also able to visit Thangafe Tso another sacred lake in the region. Nemurous beliefs and tales are associated with this lake. One of them being the sight of a beautiful Gompa with Lamas in the clear water of the lake visible only to those who have not eaten meat or non-vegetarian food for atleast three months.

Thangafe lake can be reached from KhriLam and Thongleng villages. The stiff six hours climb levels at Methchang or the lower lake. Above it is the Diuchang or middle lake and at the top Stotchang. Visitors place coloured flags and do a religious round of lake. Situated at an altitude of 14000ft these lakes are visited from June to October. We spent the night in a grazier hut beside the Methchang. We took a round of the lake early in the morning but were not fortunate to see the Gompa and the lamas in the water of the lakes, probably because we had been eating non veg meals every day.

Gorsam Chorten (Stupa) in Zimithang Valley

CHAPTER EIGHT

Guru Padamsambhava's Seats of Worship

According to the research scholars, on the invitation of Tibetan king Thisrong Dichen, Guru Padamsambhav journeyed to Tibet in the year 747 A.D. It is believed that during that period he visited Monpa and Sherdukpen areas also and sowed the seeds of Budhism in these areas. Seven places in Monpa area and nine places in Sherdukpen area are regarded, as the seats of worship of Guru Padamsambhava.

In 1967 for few nonths I was posted at Jhang. From the window of my bamboo hut a gompa was visible to the east in the background of a steep rock face. On enquiry I was told that this is "Kimnash Gompa"and at some time Guru Rimpoche - Guru Padamsambhav had perfomed penance here. The very next morning we set off for the place. After an hour's steep climb we reached there. We sat with "Komiar Lama" the care-taker Lama deputed from Tawang Gompa and over cups of yak butter salt tea got acquinted with the history of this Gompa. For the first time we came to know about other such places where Guru Padamsambhav had performed Penance, also that there is a tradition of recording the history of such places and Gompa. Such records are called Karchhak.

Kimnash means place of pilgrimage. On this spot of penance of Guru Padamshambhav, the founder of Karmapa sect Lama Rangchung Dorjee (1109-1192) constructed a Gompa. In due course many changes took place and now this gompa is of Gelugpa sect under Tawang monastery. But the rites of Ningma sect and worshipping of Guru Padamshambhav are still invogue.

The second place is Taksang Gompa which is at one day's march from Tawang via Gamra La and Shunget tser to Zimithang. Taksang Gompa is the only suitable place for night halt on way to zimithang. According to the komiar Lama and the Karchak, this Gompa was constructed earlier than Tawang Gompa. Several nights I stayed in the smoke filled room of the komiar Lama. Every time I wanted answers to my new quirries about this place. Through the local interpreter the story of Guru Padamshambhav based on Kangyur was related. The scholars of both Ningma as well as Gelugpa sects agree on this. When Lord Budha was on his death bed he had stated to his favourite disciple Anand that he will take birth as Padamshambhav and impart the knowledge of mystic Tantra. On the query that why he did not taught Tantra in his present life, Budha had said that as he had taken birth from a human womb, he is not fully qualified for this. For introducing and practice of Tantra he will take celestial birth. He further stated that for this he had to invite the deities from all ten directions as well as the past BodhiSattawa and obtain their approval. Accordingly Buddha descended on this earth as Padamsambhav on the tenth day of the fifth month. Dawa Dakpa on a lotus flower as a newborn child. Another story narrated about the re-appearance of Guru PadamShambhav is related to Riwalsar Lake.Rivalsar lake is situated 18 Kms from Mandi in Himachal Pradesh and is a sacred place for Buddhists. In his young age, this great precepter had made princess Mandarva, daughter of the king of Johar, his spiritual consort. Mandarva had also in presence of Santrakhshit, vowed to follow tantrik religion. But the king did not approve this. Guru Padamsambhav used to visit Mandarva in the palace by virtue of his tantrik power. One day the king detected it and he was caught. Guru Padamsambhav was tied to a pole, oil was poured all around him and he was set on fire. But the preceptor turned the oil in to water and the pole to which he was tied became a lotus flower. Padamsambhav was found again on the lotus flower. The king of Johar fell on his feet and offered Mandarva to him as his wife. Therefore Lake Riwalsar is one of the menifestation of the miracle of the great preceptor.

In Taksang Gompa the statue is of DORJEE Troloh, one of the manifestations of Guru Padamsambhaw. The facial expression is wrathful. But the anger is born out of compassion for all beings. In his right hand he holds a Dorjee (Vajra) symbolizing the in destructibility of Budhism. In his left hand he holds a "Phurba" symbolizing the dynamic quality of energy associated with void. Phurba is a triple bladed small dagger used as ritual instrument. The guru is standing on a pregnant tigress. This tigress is believed to be emanation of Dakini Tashi Menmo khenden, daughter of SindhuRaja, given to Guru as his spiritual consort. The pregnancey of the tigress is symbolic of the spark of knowledge and wisdom latent in all beings. Dorjee Troloh is standing on the back of the tigress, with his right leg bent and left leg extended, a posture of firmess. This firmness signify the protection extended by the Guru to the disciples and the religion.The entire figure of Dorjee Troloh is surrounded by flames of fire. Which represents the devine energy of Guru.

It is also stated that when Guru Padamsambhav was performing penance here a tiger was at his service. Stak means tiger and Sang means place. Below the Gompa on way to Zimithang along the stream on the walls of overhanging rocks there are engravings of some figures, stated to be made by devine powers. On the rocks there are imprints of foot marks of the Guru and hoof marks of his pony.

The third place is Jiksang. This is at two days march from Tawang above village Jhangda in a large meadow. During winter it is covered under snow. To reach this place another track is via Bumla and KhominLa. Near this place is Sarong Gompa. It is sand that Guru rested at this place for few days. On the rock the imprint of his palm, the place where he kept his religious books and the imprint of his back where he rested reclining on the rock can be seen. It is said that a leopard was at his service here. Jik means leopard and Sang means place. Later on Sarong Gompa was constructed here.

When the invasion of Dukpa sect on Tawnag increased. Mera Lama asked the Lamas to take up sword in self defense. Among the warrior Lamas was one Lama Phuntso DakPa. After the invasion was over Lama Phuntso Dakpa thought it proper to repent the killings made even for the sake of religion. He went to Tibet. There in SERA monastery he spent his days studying the religious scripts. For many years he stayed with a scholar Lama Yeh Khajowo Tendawa. On realizing the deep sense of repentance in Lama Phuntso DakPa, he told him to go back to Mon region at Jiksang Jawa, construct a Gompa there, and spent his time in meditation there. This will redeem him from his sense of repentance. After death he will be reborn to expand the religion. Lama Phuntso DakPa constructed Sarong Gompa and is known as Sarong Rimpoche.

When Lama Phuntso Dakpa was returning from Tibet he stayed at Sarteng Gompa above village Sokchen. One day when, he was in meditation he saw a fearsome snake approaching him. Lama Phuntso DakPa threw his rosary on the snake. The snake changed into a human form and introduces himself as 'SERTENG SIDA' the patron God of the region. He predicted full success in the project of Lama Phuntso Dakpa and also that he may construct the Gompa wherever he wants but every time he will be reborn in this region only. It is believed that Sarong Rimpoche reborns every time in Pangchen region. The people of Pangchen do not kill snake. They consider them incarnation of Lamas.

The present Sarong Rimpoche is the sixth incarnation. Tawang monastery has a permanent seat for Sarong Rimpoche.

The fourth place is in the west of SELA ridges at BANGAJHANG. At an altitude of about 13000ft there is a Gompa and a natural Lake. All around these are numerous stone symbols. People visit this place from July to October. From November to June the place is covered in snow.

Twice I Passed through this area but could not find opportunity to stay for the night. It was narrated by a number of people that during October, on a cloudless, clear moonligt night, one can see a number of lamps burning inside the lake. To observe this miracle the third time I stayed for the night in the room adjacent to the Gompa. The villagers had stacked enough dry firewood. At night we saw the scene of burning lamps inside the lake. There was a mild breeze causing waves on the surface of the clear azure water of the lake. The waves starting from the shore and breaking in the middle of the lake reflected the stars and moonlight. This created an illusion of small burning lamps and these extinguishing in the lake. The location of the lake is such that the winds effect is from all directions. Therefore the waves starts from the shore and break in the middle of the lake. This place is now easily accessible due to construction of road up to Chhabra La.

The fifth Place TERMA BUMGAN is six Kms south of Tawang near Vill - Poidar. Here on the stone one can see the imprint of the foot mark, cap, hand and begging bowl of Guru Padamsambhava. Terma Bumgon Gompa was constructed here.

The sixth place is BHEEGA Gompa five Kms below Tawang and 500 mtrs from the road. The Gompa is situated in such a place that it can't be seen from anywhere. The small Gompa is beside a stream in the Jungle. The very place gives an eerie feeling. Below on the rock face along the River there are imprints of hand, foot, knee and cap of Guru Padamsambhav.

The seventh place is a cave, KOME PHUK ten Kms south. The entrance to the cave is very narrow. It is said that while Guru Padamsambhav was sitting in meditation in the cave a serpent came crawling towards him. The precepeter, seeing the serpent lifted himself up in the same position. His head struck the roof of the cave and made a round hole in the cave roof. Now the cave gets the sun light from this hole. On the floor there is a line indicating the crawling of the serpent.

Besides these seven places, the statue of all the eight manifestation of Guru Padamshamhav are in CHANG PRONG Gompa, six Kms below Tawang. These statues are:

i. Guru Doorjee Troloh - This is in Taksang Gompa also.

ii. Guru Senge DRADO - ferocious face with a crown of five human skulls, third eye on the forehead and elephant hide on the body..

iii. Guru Nima Ujer: - a trident in hand, with three human skull, Damru, Phan and Darchang. The Tantrik baton is called KHATANGA. In his left hand a sun - symbol and tiger skin on body.

iv. Lopon Pema Jungme - Benevolent face, Damru in right hand and Norbu in left hand.

v. Guru Pechung Yabyum: - Dorjee in right hand, left hand embracing YUB the female consort. Both the legs of YUB is around the waist of the preceptor. Yabyum is the physical symbolism of spiritual form of two in mystic unity. This posture is called PEMEKLINTAK

vi. Guru Pema GyalPo - Damru in right hand and left hand holding a mirror called 'MELONG' in which the preceptor can see the three realms of the Universe.

vii. Guru Loden Chhoksi - In padamasan, begging bowl in left hand, right hand raise in the posture of blessing.

viii. Guru Sakya Senge - The lion of Sakya dynasty. Gautam Budha.

The statue of eight manifestations of Guru Padamsamhav are duly worshipped in these two Gompas Sangeling and Changprong near Tawang as both these Gompa belong to Ningma sect.

According to local myth there was a large pond (Chang) here in which there lived a man - eater aquatic demon. In ancient time a Lama Kumdo Sange Hisi came here from Lhobra in Tibet. He made a drain, took out the water from the pond and killed that demon. He made a Gompa here and established the tutelary deity Gombuli NakPo (Goddess Kali). This Gompa is also Called Samden Chholing Gompa. According to the beliefs of Peling sub-sect of NingmaPa the statue of Guru Padamsambhav is installed here.

Now the Gompa is being looked after by Lama Pema Khandu and his whole family live in the house constructed by the side of the Gompa. In this area on some stones foot imprint of Lama Kumdo Sange Hisi and of his dog are found. Among other sacred items with Lama Pema Khandu, there is the upper portion of the skull of Lama Kumdo sange Hisi, on which is engraved the Tibtan letter "OM". It is said that during his life time, the lama got this letter om on his skull by vitue of his tantrik will power

On his death after cremation the upper portion of the skull was kept in the Gompa for ritual purposes. Now this is with Lama Pemkhandu and can be seen on specific auspicious occasion. Late Lama Kumdo senge Hisi is also addressed as JA RELPA. He is supposed to be ancestors of GonPapa clan of Dirang village.

The myth of sojourn of Guru Padamsambhav is also prevalent in Rupa, Sherdukpen area. According to the Lamas and other knowledgeable persons of this area there are nine places revered as the seat of Guru Padamsambhav. Seven places are in the radius of fifteen kms from Rupa where as two are in the foot hills of Assam.

The first place is FluJima, 2Kms west of Rupa where on the rock there are imprint of his dog's paw and a hole where he put his walking stick.

The second place is Machulu, 5 Kms west of Rupa. Here also on the rock are imprints of his foot as well as the paw of his dog and the niche in which he kept his bow and arrow.

5 Kms. east of Rupa Jambring is the third place. The myth states that here when he was resting the villagers offered him "Nik", flour made out of the dry pith of a tree of palm species, popularly known as Rangbang. He accepted their offer and threw some flour on the ground as offering to deities. This flour fell by the side of the stream and now there is a grove of Rangbang trees. In and around Rupa no where are the Rangbang trees.

The fourth seat is 6 Kms east from Rupa towards Tenga valley called Khanggishi. Here a stone resembles the shape of sherdukpen tribes shoe. It is said that this is the fossilized shoe of the preceptor.

The fifth and sixth places are in the foot hills of Assam called Jakhung and Pemaloso. Pemaloso is a rock on the confluence of Dojibuti mountain stream and Gabru River. On the rock there is an engraved lotus flower. It is said that when the preceptor was staying here the flower came on the rock on its own.

The seventh and eighth places are Urmeyan Pemagom, 15 Kms from Rupa towards Jigaon and Chupit at four and half Km from Rupa. Here on a rock at a height of six feet are the palm imprint of the preceptor.

Approximately five Kms. South from Rupa is the ninth place called Shrah -HA-Noma. The popular myth is that a demon in the guise of a wild goat attacked the preceptor. The preceptor hit him on the head with a stone shot from his bow, due to which blood (HA) gushed out and made a long trail (Noma) when the demon ran away.

In Bomdila, Dirang and Tawang areas small or large image of Guru Padamsambhav is found in every Gompa. The thin moustache on the face and Khatanga in hand helps in recognizing the preceptor. Many more myths came to knowledge during my long stay which convinces one to believe that Guru Padamsambhav must have visited these places.

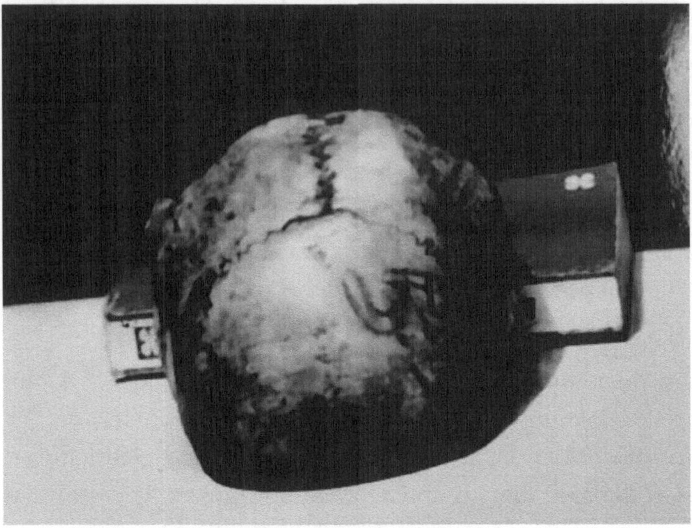

Skull of Lam Kumdo Sange Hisi with "Om" letter of Tibetan Script.

CHAPTER NINE

Ani Gompa

Ani Gompa is one of the prominent GomPa in Tawang area. Like the MonPa boys the MonPa girls also get initiated in nuns hood and live like Boudh - Bhikshuni.

For the first time I saw a group of these Ani in Tawang. A mixed group of old, middle aged, young women and girls. The first sight revoked a feeling of amazement and then a sense of pity overwhelmed my heart. Tonsured head, bare wrists, and covered in dark maroon loose habits, this group of ten to twelve nuns had come from Gyanggong Ani Gompa to Tawang Gompa for collection of food grains. During the construction of Tawang Gompa, the sister of Mera Lama, who had already become a nun, this Ani Gompa was constructed for her. Now about sixty two nuns are residing in this Gompa. The internal administration of this Ani Gompa is in the hands of a senior nun. Appointment of such administrator from among the senior nuns is for a period of three years.

The genesis of "Bhikshuni Sangh" took place in sixth century when Budha himself initiated his foster mother, the sister of his late mother along with five hundred women in nun's hood. Budha differentiated progressive Budhism from orthodox Brahmanism by his, this decision. It is said that lord Budh considered the aspect that if women who are the pivotal element of family and society, shall come in to 'Sangh' forsaking their conjugal and maternal responsibilities, the very infrastructure of the society will shatter. But the progressive Buddhist thinking could not disappoint the assembly of women who had walked from Kapilvastu to Vaishali seeking Bodhisattawa and salvation.

Through the interpreter we tried to know the routine inside the nunnery from the incharge Ani. All our questions were replied in very soft and affectionate sentences. The training of nuns is arduous. To achieve nun hood twenty six essential conditions are there such as physically and mentally healthy, balanced temper, patience even in distress, not to be in family way etc. Throughout their life to abstain from lie, stealing, intoxicants, marriage, and observe celibacy. Everyday study the religious texts and spend time in prayer and performing laid down religious rituals of the Gompa. Like the boys the girls are also taken as Geyen but above that there is no provision for them to achieve the grade of Getsul and Galong. For their livelihood they visit the villages in group of two-three for collecting alms. The villagers respectfully give them food grains and money. The collected alms are then brought to the common pool in the Gompa. The group of Ani visit villages in Tawnag, Dirang and Bomdila areas. These girls accept the life of Ani voluntarily and on the consent of their parents, and not under any coercion. Even after becoming an Ani they help and participate in the activities of their family. Village and the society if required. The mentality of escapism and inaction is not found in them. The hard labour and dedication with which they work in the maintenance of their Gompa, carry 20 to 30 Kgs weight of food grains collected from the villages and live on frugal diet is ample proof of their sacrifice and faith. On getting sickness, they prefer to be treated with local herbs and medicines.

The life of Ani is a natural one for the MonPa girls. It is in no way abnormal. The unorthodox Buddhist Philosophy do not hinder the return of any Ani in the family life leaving nunhood. According to the norms of Gyanggong Ani Gompa, a nun wishing to return to family life has to present herself infront of the abbbot of Tawang monastery, beg forgiveness and permission to get married. This system is called "SHAKPA." On acceptance of her request the abbot grant her the permission to leave and to make an offer of some cash and food grain to the Gompa, The Cash amount may be from Rs 500/- to Rs 1000/-. After this the Ani can get married and live in society honorably. In some cases if the Ani out of embarrassment, do not want to appear in person, her guardian and relatives may appear before the abbot with the request and offer of ShakPa. There are some instances of a Lama marrying an Ani, leaving the life of monastery and leading family life in villages. These lamas are called DROLO. There is no restriction if a village youth sought to marry an Ani on getting her consent. In such cases the youth himself pay the amount of Shakpa to the Gompa. This type of marriage is considered more honorable than a Lama marrying an Ani. The Marriage between a Lama and Ani is not appreciated. Such nuptial is called DAMYANG KHATE means the decline of two initiated persons. But overtly the society accept them and assist them in leading a normal life.

There is no Ani Gompa in west Kameng district. There are five Ani Gompas in Tawang district. The oldest and largest one is Gayanggong Ani Gompa. Near by is the Brahmdochhung Ani Gompa, in which there are forty Ani. The third Ani Gompa is above vill - Lhou on way to Brakar Gompa, Sugsur phu Ani Gompa, which has about thirty Ani. The fourth Ani Gompa is at Eiwang above village - Thongleng. There are about twenty five Ani in this Gompa. In this

Gompa two Lamas also stay. The remaining Ani Gompas are visited by Lamas for performing religious rituals but do not stay there at night. The fifth Ani Gompa is above village - Namet on way to KhromtinGompa called Shermang Ani Gompa. All thes Ani Gompas are situated away from the villages in wilderness. In and around the Ani Gompa are small dwellings made of stones and timber. Gyanggong Ani Gompa is supported by Tawang Gompa but the remaining four Gompas sustain on the alms given by the villages and collected by the Ani. They have got their own NeyerPa and Umdze and the system of ShakPa is performed before them.

It is also seen that divorcee, widows and unmarried mothers can also become an Ani, there is no age restriction. But once becoming an Ani, the rule of Shakpa is to be followed for returning to family life.

CHAPTER TEN

Dobley, Khromtien and Lhageyala Gompas.

The story of the construction of these three Gompas in Kameng is very interesting and related to each other. While Dobley and Khromtien Gompas are situated in Lumla and Tawnag, Lhageyala Gompa is at a distance of 53 Kms south west from Bomdila above village Morsing.

Three Lamas of Tawang monastery Lama Kheyan, Lama Sonam Gyachen and Lama Eshigele went to Tibet to complete their studies. On conclusion of their studies the Panchen Lama called them and said that they should proceed for Tawang only after narrating to him their dreams which they may get on the previous night of their departure for Tawang.

In compliance to the orders of the Panchen Lama the three Lamas presented themselves before him. Lama Kheyan narrated that in his dream he saw several precious items and a beautiful River of clear water flowing in the base of a mountain.

Lama Sonam stated, that in his dream he saw heap of raw meat kept in layers.

Lama Eshigeyele said that in his dream he found himself sitting in meditation on a high hill. A beautiful devine female came to him and offered him a bowl full of milk in which a drop of blood was floating.

The dream of Lama Eshigele according to some other Lamas is that three devine females came to him and offerd him a bowl full of milk in which a red coral was kept. Yet another version narrated to me that Lama Eshigele found himself sitting in the lap of a divine female who was offering him a bowl full of milk.

The Panchen Lama after listening to their dream said to Lama Kheyan that he will construct a Gompa in Monpa area on a high feature overlooking many villages and a fertile valley. He will be reborn again and his incarnations will be the abbot of this Gompa and continue to propogate the religious work.

Lama Kheyan returned from Lhasa. On the high feature above Lumla he received some devine indication and he saw that from this height the many villages of DakPoTsogeyat area and their green fields are visible. Lama Kheyan constructed a Gompa at this height which is known as Dobley Gompa. In this Gompa the statue of Awalokiteshwar of thousand hands, eyes and eleven heads was established. The Gompa is situated amongst dense forest and the climb from Lumla to the Gompa takes two hours. Adjacent to the Gompa is the residence of Dobley Rimpoche. There are few huts also in which the visiting Ani and Pilgrims can stay for the night. Fire-wood and water is available in plenty here.

During my stay at Lumla, I visited Dobley Gompa on several occasions. Every time on the bidding of DobleyRimpoche, spent the night there. I used to converse with the tall and well built Dobley Rimpoche in Hindi. But his limited ability in Hindi conversation used to come in way while answering my several quarries. Then it was compelling to seek the help of an interpreter. On arrival at Dobley Gompa, the Rimpoche affectionately used to offer a seat, then pick up the ornate amulet made of brass and copper and touch it on my forehead with incantation of some mantra. After that he used to offer a spoon full of Ara from the bowl made of human skull rimmed with silver on my palm to sip and the round of yak butter salt tea would go on. The night I used to spent in the adjacent room. Inspite of my tiredness I used to get up at 4 o'clock in the morning and braving the cold come to enjoy the hypnotic scenery. At the far distance the ocher sky at the SELA ridges and the rising sun behind it looked out so enchanting. Infront the three peaks of chong chongma, and the changing blue colour of the mountain ridges gradually becoming green as the sunlight fell on them. Down below the villages Lumla, Magnam, Hungla and beyond Tawangchu the villages Bompa and Bongleng. In the west across Namjang chu the clear views of villages Bletting and Muktur. After some time the mist rising from Tawang chu used to cover the villages. After that there remained the boundless sea of white mist and at the far end the three peaks of Chong Chongma. The call of komiar lama used to bring me back from this hypnotic spell. After getting fresh I used to visit the Gompa and sometime sit in the back row of the Lamas when the morning Prayer was recited by them row. The collective voice of Lamas used to rise -

Lama La Kepso Chiyu
Sange La Kepso Chiyu
Che La Kepso Chiyu
Gedon La Kepso Chiyu

At one occasion some Lamas with deep concentration and in deep voice were reciting a prayer. On giving a concentrated attention a few Sanskrit words came to me. The vibration caused in the atmosphere was very grave and created an eerie feeling. During lunch, on my constant request a Lama explained to me that this Mantra is for invoking Dorjee Sempa and it is called Hikgya because there are one hundred words init. He recited the mantra slowly for my benefit:

Om BA Jar Sato SA MA YA MA DU PA
LA YA BA JAR SATO TENO PA TRIK
THA DRI DO ME BA WA SU TO KHAIYO
ME BA WA SU PO KHAIYO ME BA WA
AH NU RA KTO ME BA WA SAR WA SI
THI ME PRA YA CHA SAR WA KARMA
SU CHA ME CHITTAK SIRI YAM KURU
HUNG HA HA HA HA HI BA GA WA NA
SAR WA TATHAGATO BA JAR MA ME
MUN CHA BA JAR BA WA MASAMAYA SATO
HA HUNG PHAT.

Possibly the incantation is of the mantra OM VAJRA SATWA BHAGWAN SARV TATHAGAT VAJRA etc of which letter is pronounced separately. Whatever is the meaning of this mantra the collective incantation by Lamas used to create an eerie effect.

Dobley Rimpoche was invited in government functions also. On 25 January 1972 the inauguration of new administrative centre at village- MUKTO was conducted by him. In 1981-82 when I visited Dobley Gompa, Dobley Rimpoche was not there. It was told that the Rimpoche is living some where else becoming a DRULO. Due to his, this action, he has been debarred to occupy the seat of Dobley Rimpoche at Tawang monastery.

Lama Sonam Geyachen was instructed by Pangchen Lama to construct a Gompa in Monpa area and that he would attain Nirvan after that and would not be reborn. Lama Geyachen came to Monpa area and was in search of a suitable site. He made his temporary shelter on GeshiLa. In the Jungle he found a dog leading him. At one place the dog vanished. Lama Geyachen took it a devine indication and resolved to construct a Gompa at that site. But due to a steep standing rock the site was not large enough to construct a Gompa. By virtue of his spiritual power he pushed the steep standing rock putting his both hands and head on it and got enough space to construct the Gompa. Khromtien Gompa was constructed on this site. To day also on that rock the imprint of his head and hands are visible. This also means layers of raw meat. SA-meat, KHAR Layers.

The 12Kms. Climb to khromtein Gompa starts from village - Namet. The climb is gradual up to Sherteng Gompa. From Sherteng Gompa to Shermang Ani Gompa the climb is difficult. After taking rest. rest at Shermang Ani Gompa we resumed the march ahead.

In Shermang Ani Gompa there is the statue of JAMBA. The steep path after this goes through jungle over the rocks up to Chuchu me che Mane. It is said that at this location the dog had attracted the attention of Lama Geyachen by making the sound Chu Chu. Therefore the Mane is called Chu Chu MECh e. The path becomes easy after this mane. The Khromtien Gompa is situated among green beautiful Juniper trees and thin bamboo grooves called DUNG. Inside the Gompa is the statue of lama Sonam Geyachen made of clay. There are also statue of Dorjee Changtong and Sakhar Geyeen. In the wall cupboards are kept the religious text of Domang and Dorchoyee. The pillars are decorated with antique swords, spears and shields made of Rhino hide. To the east of the Gompa amids thick forest is the place surrounded with large rocks where Lama Geyachen had made his temporary shelter. Now with the gompa there are three rooms and a kitchen where the villagers coming to this Gompa stay for the night. From Khromtein. Gompa one can see the entire Tawang area. The upkeep of this Gompa is under Tawang monastery.

After listening to the dream stated by Lama Eshigele, Panchen Lama had directed him to construct a Gompa near the plains of India on a high hill below which a River would be flowing. Also that he would take re-birth and his incarnation would propogate the religion. The drop of blood in the milk bowl indicates that. His one incarnation would lead a family life while the other would remain a celibate. This would be an exception in Gelugpa sect.

Lama Eshigele came on foot from Bomdila while proceeding toward plains of Assam and stayed in village-Morsing. One day wondering in search of a suitable site, and getting tired he sat on a hill to rest and fell asleep. A white bird came and flew away taking his cap. Lama Eshigele walked in the direction of the bird's flight. The bird sat on a high feature with his cap. When he reached there the bird flew away leaving his cap there. Lama Eshigele took it as a devine indication and with the help of villagers constructed a Gompa.

It is stated that after the construction of this Gompa the followers of DukPa sect from the bordering area of Bhutan invaded and tried to demolish this Gompa. But the local demons and ethereal powers took form of ferocious wild animals and frightened away the invaders. The many stones on way to Gompa resemble the figures of wild animals.

In 1968 we had marched on foot from Dirang to Lhageyela Gompa via Mandala Phudung, Domkho, Morsing and Kalaktang. Now a road has been constructed connecting Kalaktang with Bomdila. One can now travel by road from Bomdila to Kalaktang, stay for the night in the inspection banglow at Kalaktang and make a sojourn to LhaGeyela Gompa. The path up to Morsing is along the River. After that the serpentine track goes climbing the steep hill. The Gompa is situated on a rock feature amidst thick forest. From there below the entire Kalktang area and the villages Sanglam, Morsing and Domkho are visible. To the west is international boundary with Bhutan and across visible are the villages in Bhutan. From Kalaktang one can go to Bhairav Kund and Udalguri in Assam.

The present Lhageyela Rimpoche is the eight incarnation in the line and was born in village - Lish in Dirang area. The meaning of Lhageyela is the temple of one hundred Devine statues.

Khromtin Gompa

Caretaker Lama of Khromtien Gompa

CHAPTER ELEVEN

Thimbu-Mago-Poto

The vista of natural scenic beauty delights and stimulates the heart. When ever I gazed towards north cast from Jhang, the brightness of Thimbu glacier looked inviting. In October the blue sky was dotted with white clouds. This was a suitable season for trekking. We started for Thimbu Mago region with our guide Dawa Norbu of village - Mukto. After getting dawn to Tawangchu River the steep climb, to village Shroh was quite tiring and we stayed in the village Gompa. In the evening the care-taker Ani of the Gompa came with a kettle of SingChhang and wooden cup. The affectionate repeated request of her forced us to accept her hospitability. I had by now sampled Bang Chhang of most of the MonPa villages but Singchhang of this village, was superb in comparison. After this whenever we came to this direction the SingChang of vill- Shroh made us stay here.

From Shroh we came to Broksar and spent the night in a log cabin made amidst pine forest and on third day reached village - Thimbu. In the end of our march the climb from Tawangchu to village Thimbu was again very tiring. We stayed in the house of the GaonBura as there was no staging hut in the village. At that time there were eighteen houses here. The livelihood of the village depended on yak and sheep rearing. Any type of agricultural cultivation was considered a taboo here. The next day also we spent in the village and interacted with them with the help of our guide and interpreter, Dawa Norbu. In afternoon two hunters of the village brought a mountain goat. When they came to know our plan to go to Mago via Takar- Phuk, they suggested us to go via Ongong La - Lorang Chu and Chigyap La. We accepted their suggestion out of our curiosity to trek on a new route. We started early morning. After walking three kms east from vill- Thimbu the path turns to north and the climb to Ongongla starts. After four hours we were climbing down to Lorang Chu crossing Ongong La. There was a bridge on Lorang Chu. The valley was covered with Rhodondron bushes and among them large flocks of Pheasants were seen moving. Even the Munal were seen in large numbers. After crossing Lorangchu on way towards Chigyap La we rested for Lunch and tea. From this place also we enjoyed the movements of the flocks of colourful pheasants. By late afternoon we were at the top of Chigyap La. The ochre sunlight had enveloped Chigyap La. We sat there to take rest and got engrossed in the panorma of sun-set oblivious of the approaching darkness. When we came to realize this we hurried down towards Mago. Half way down the track the darkness engulfed everything and without a flash -light we stumbled any how over village Niyuri. On hearing our foot-falls the large mastif dogs of the village started barking. We stopped over the village in darkness scared of these mastiffs. Dawa Norbu started calling the villagers to restrain the dogs. After half an hour two villagers with burning torches of green pine wood came up to escort us to the village. We came to the house of the GaonBura and after accepting his hospitality of yak butter salt tea marched two kms to our post at Topgey.

In Mago area there are only these two villages -Niyuri and Diyuri. The distance between these two villages is approximately of one Kms. The River Tawang Chu flows by the side of the village as a narrow stream. The livelihood of these villages is yak and sheep rearing. They do not have any aptitude towards agriculture. There are hot water springs by the side of Tawangchu between the village Topgey. A few springs have boiling hot water. But the water in two springs are bearable and these have been walled by stones and covered by pine planks for bathing purposes.

The apparel of the people of Mago is distinct from the dress of Monpas of Tawang. In their headgear of yak hair in place of five downward pointing fingers, there are many strings of yak hair protruding like a cobweb around the head. This headgear is worn by male and females both and this make their appearance distinct from Tawang MonPas. The females also adorn themselves with two strings of red and yellow coral beads which hang from each ear to the waist band. Their dialect is also a mixture of Tibetan and monpa words. Inspite of being followers of Budhism there is no Gompa in these two villages. There was no literate person in these two villages. But by nature they were no less hospitable and humble than other people of this region.

After staying for three days we resumed our trekking to Lungar and Thulung La. From Topgey to Lungar the trek is a gradual climb along Tawangchu up to Chuna. The name Chuna gave an impression of a heap of white lime but it was just opposite to that. The local name of this place is "ChhuNag". Chhu means water and Nag means black. The place of black water. Here the stream flows over-black sand and slate stones looking dark. The climb from Lungar to ThulungLa is very steep. One has to stop for recovering ones breathing at every three hundred meters. The Thulung La pass at 17000' is the boundary between Bharat and Tibet. We returned back to Topgey after surveying the area in and around ThulungLa.

In the morning while walking form Topgey to Lungar near Chuna we had seen a number of burrows on the even surface of hill slope. We waited silently and saw large size yellow colour rodent like animals coming out from the holes who sat outside with their both hands raised. They used to make sharp whistling noise and get inside one burrow, and come out from other. The locals call them "Chhipka." The whole show was very funny. These animals are found in these remote mountains at the height of 12000ft. In winter from November to May they hibernate underground in their burrows. During that period their heart and pulse beat become very slow and they do not require any food and water. These harmless and playful creatures are also being hunted in large numbers every year. The meat of these animals is odorous and unedible but the skin and fat are used by the locals as the medicine for treatment of pain in joints and especially for pain in the waist.

In this area besides these "Chhipkas" there are mountain sheep and white snow leopard with black round spot on their hide.

On our return to Mago, we met few villagers from village Luguthang, who had come to seek medical aid for the epidemic of blood-dysentery in their village. We along with S.S.B. Jawans and Para-Medic accompanied them to their village crossing Chere La and Gorung Chu. After Gorung Chu the climb to Thukur La at 17000ft was very torturous. At the pass we braved strong icy winds. Climbling down we reached the village. This village of 17-18 houses is situated at the altitude of 12000 ft. The livelihood of this village is also sheep and yak rearing. There was no sign of literacy and modernization. Being Buddhist they do not kill any animal but consume the meat of dead animals. The blood dysentery affected them after consuming the meat of a yak carcass. The sense of even normal sanitation was absent. With the Jawans of S.S.B, we started the cleaning of the village, making trench Latrines, getting the nails of their fingers cut and washing their hands in the solution of Potassium Permagnent every time they came after relieving themselves. The sick were administered medicines and oral liquid solutions to save them from de-hidration. Within twelve hours we were successful in controlling the epidemic. The death toll till we reach there was of two children and one old woman. It was seen that as these people seldom take any medicine, even the small dose given to them was proving effective. After spending two nights in the village we returned to Gorung Chu again crossing Thukar La. The SSB Jawans and medics took leave to go to Topgey Camp and we decided not to return to Jhang but to go to Dirang.

The trek from GorungChu go to LAP meadow and gradually climbs to Che La. We found a number of yak graziers hut along the stream in Lap meadow. The wall of these low roofed huts are made of stones and on the roof crudely hewn pine planks were kept. Inside there a stone hearth, beside that thick pine planks flooring and niches in the wall to keep their belongings. The meadow LAP belong to village - Thembang of Dirang area. After coming some distance we came across the villagers of Thembang whose yaks, sheep and ponies were seen everywhere in this meadow. We halted for the night in one of the yak -graziers hut. After putting off our rucksacks we came out to interact with the Brokpas. These graziers who spend the whole summer season in high attitude meadows with yaks, sheep and ponies are called BrokPas in local dialect. Their dress constitute of leather Jackets, leather leggings, and yak hair cap. Their family members keep them adequately supplied with Tsampa, Chhang, Ara, salt and of local tea. The yak butter and Cheese are their staple diet. These Brokpas living in the lap of nature are found always smiling, happy, humble and very hospitable. In the evening every one gets busy in milching the yaks, securing the calfs in enclosures and looking after their mastiffs. Inspite of their busy routine they offered us fresh yak cheese and salt tea. Some Brokpas had come form kimiya La. Most of the huts had good stock of leather bags full of yak butter ad cheese.

Next day we got up at four o'clock in the morning and finished our morning rituals. Outside the deep tranquility of the meadow surrounded with high mountain peaks and the sound of bells hanging from the neck of yaks was an unique experience. We resumed our march and by five-thirty we were ascending Che La at 15000ft. After only one hours climb we felt tiredness and out of breath which forced us to rest. About eight o'clock crossing Che-La we were at another large meadow POTO and by the side of a beautiful lake there. On the other side of the lake a large herd of sheeps were grazing. From Poto we could see to the east the hill ridges going down covered in thick blue black forest. Towards north and west were the high mountains and our path towards south over Chhang La, Pang La and Poshing La to Thungri.

While resting at Poto I recalled some portion of the tour diary of a veteran officer of the then NEFA. He had mentioned that in 1913 captain E.F. Bailey along with Capt Morsehead, a surveyor, had returned from Tibet taking a route straight from North to south and after crossing ThulungLa had reached Thembang via Che La and poshingLa. From this place the valley between SELA and

Bomdial is clearly visible. In 1962 the invading Chinese troops had taken this Bailey track to bypass our defenses at SELA and had reached Dirang and Thembang. From POTO we crossed PangLa and PoshingLa and reached Chhang La at an altitude of 11000ft. After crossing Chhangla, down below we found two graziers hut and decided to spend the night in one of them. But we found both the huts occupied by villagers from Thembang. In one of the hut was the Gaonbura of Thembang Ngoichung with his two men. He invited us to share the space in the hut. We slept early being tired. Next morning the sky was clouded. We resumed our journey inspite of light rain. The track is over a narrow ridge and gradually desecends to Thungri. From this ridge to the east is the dense forest of Miji area and to the west thick Jungle of Monpa area. It took us five hours to reach the Assam Rifles post at Thungri where a Naib-subedar welcomed us. At night we confered with him about the routes and terrain and decided to go to Miji area via villages Pangma. Lhachang encercling village Thembang from below and coming to village BUT and proceeding to NAFRA. Next morning we took leave of Assam Rifles men and by evening reached Lhachhang via Pangma. Our guide from Thungri was Sange Monpa of village Namshu. Lhachhang was a small hamlet of Namshu villagers which they had inhabited founding fertile agricultural land there.

Early morning next day we started our journey. By noon we were in village But. The Monpas of these villages - But, Khoitam, Rahung and Jiri are also Budhisht but have also retained the rituals of their previous faith. This makes them different from the MonPas of Dirang. Their dialect and way of living are also different. Therefore the main Monpas call themselves "NangPa" and the But Monpas "Chhipa".

After lunch we left But for Nafra. The trees in the forest along the track were full of orchids. Many species of Dendrobium and Cibribidium orchids are found here. The path up to Nafra is easy. By dusk we were at Nafra and spent the night in a hut by the bank of Bichom River. Next day moved along River Bichom and reached the Miji village Dichik and halted in a vacant hut outside the village.

Initially the villagers looked upon us suspiciously. Two villagers came down and wanted to know the purpose of our visit in mixed Hindi-Assamese broken sentences. We introduced ourselves and offered them Bidi, cigarettes and match boxes. This pacified them and a young man volunteered to guide us up to BULU.

We resumed our march next day with the guide. The track along Bichom River was through thick forest, muddy and full of Leeches and snakes. From Dichik we came to Dibbin. From Dibbin the track followed a tributary of Bichom called Difri River. We reached Bulu passing village Mathau. Bulu was a hamlet of only three huts. The Miji live in huts made of bamboo and banana leaves for one year and then construct another such hut. We found an abondoned hut. The hut was infested with spiders and all sorts of insects which we cleared by torching them. We spent the night in the hut. Our guide had returned to vill- Mathau leaving us near Bulu. We found a middle aged person sitting infront of a hut and weaving a cane basket. We went near him but there was no response from him. Inspite of his missing index finger of right hand he was deftly weaving the cane basket. Two women and three small children were squatting at some distance. One of our companions Tamding Wangchuk asked him something in Monpa dialect which he replied in Monpa dilect. But we were glad to know that now we can interact with him in

MonPa dialect. We offered him Match box, cigarette and biscuits to the children and sat with them. During the discourse he explained that he often visits Dirang with his cane baskets and other cane items and get his requirement of essential goods in exchange. He told us that a track goes to the west through thick forest which comes up on the ridge between Thungri and Chhangla. This track is seldom frequented therefore gets covered by undergrowth. To indicate the track there are indications cut on the tree trunks to prevent straying. Bulu was at a height of 5000ft. whereas Thungri- ChhangLa ridge has an average height of 11000ft.

Early morning we marched from Bulu. The climb started through dense bamboo groves. The so called path was covered with almost two feet humus of rotten leaves and infested with thousands of leeches. The thick canopy of trees prevented the sun rays. As we gained height the bamboo forest remained behind and came the rhodendron and pine trees. After marching for ten hours with a break for lunch we came up on the ridge- at about 3 o'clock in the afternoon. We took the right turn on the ridge and reached in the same grazier hut down ChhangLa from where we had started seven days back. From ChhangLa we reached Mago and completed the circle of our sojourn.

MonPa Women Mago area

CHAPTER TWELVE

The Beautiful Valley of Dirang and Sangti

Coming out of the cold, rain and fog of Bomdila the view after fifteen km down becomes enchanting. Another road bifurcates from here towards Salari agricultural farm and goes to Nafra via But and Jirigaon. The main metalled road goes up to Tawang taking sharp turns through Munna camp, Dirang village, Dirang administrative centre, Senge, Baishkhi and over SELA.

Dirang village is situated at a high ground on the confluence of Dirang Ri and Sangti Ri. A number of rivulets originate from Dorshee Broh meadow on the southern slope of Bangajhang ridge. These rivulets coming together become a mountain River. In this meets a large mountain stream coming down from Saktang between village Senge and Nyukmadong. This River is known by names as Mebang Ri, Dirang Ri and Dirang Gong ri. Sangti Ri meet this River from north-west. The origin of Sangti Ri is from POTO. Dirang Ri meets Bichom River passing through Munna camp, Salari farm down Nafra.

The prominent villages of this area are Dirang, Thembang and Namshu. Other villages are Khoitam, Rahung, Ewang, Lish, Lubrang, chug, Nyukmadong and

Senge. In Sangti valley the villages are Sangti, Khalibok, Phudung, khaso, and Lhachhang. Slightly apart are villages Lagam and Pangma. In Dirang village along the road there is a long Mane constructed in the memory of the members of twelve families of this village who were killed by the armed men from Tibet in perhaps nineteenth century when they opposed the construction of a Dzong, a small fortress in the village by them.

Budhism Came to this area in the end of eighteen century. Prior to that the people were animist and believing in Ghosts and other ethereal powers. To please them animals sacrifice was in vogue. With the advent of Budhism the people of Dirang came to know that wherever Budhism has been adopted the influence of these ethereal powers have vanished. They sent their representative to Tashi Lhunpu monastery in Tibet to Panchen Lama. The panchen Lama sent Lama Drekong Rimpoche of karmapa sect to Dirang. On reaching Dirang Drekong Rimpoche established Budhism and removed the fear of all evil powers. The Budhism came to this village after the construction of Tawang monastery.

There is the popular myth about an encounter of Drekong Rimpoche with a ferocious demon who used to live in a huge black rock inside the village. Drekong Rimpoehe killed that demon and smashed the black rock beneath the earth. The first Buddhist Gompa of Dirang was constructed at this place and the statue of Drekong Rempoche was established in this. A stone piece of the size 8"x 4" is also kept here said to be the fossilized heart of the demon. The irregular cut marks on the one end of the stone is said to be the marks of the sword of Drekong Rimpoche.

In this area the influence of karmapa and Ningmapa sects came first. Gradually the influence of Gelugpa took over from the regime of second Dalai Lama. The other gompas which were constructed in this village are khachikpa gompa of Peling sub sect patronized by gonpapa clan of this village. This is related to the Chang Prong Gompa of Tawang area. Above the village the largest gompa is Rimphokpa gompa which was got constructed by a monpa Lama addressed as Lama Khan or Rim phokpa Lama. He had achieved his spiritual powers in Gueme monastery of Tibet. In this gompa the ritual of konchho-chhindu and Gelugpa both the sects are in vogue. The fourth is of Gelugpa sect Gompa Lhakhang. The fifth is Lihung gompa and the sixth kharsadung gompa. The kharsadung gompa is also called kangyur Lhakhang as the 108 volumes of kangyur are preserved here.

The monpas of Dirang have several different clans. The prominent are Gonpapa, Merakpa; Chhumkhapa, Phyichhunpa, Jamchhunpa, Dungkharpa, Serthipa and Bagipa, The people of Eiwang village are Raktipa and originally belong to Dirang. Marriage within ones clan is prohibited.

Ten kms to the north-east is the Sangti valley and Sangti village. The gravel road goes along Sangati Ri. On the entrance of the valley government sheep breeding farm is situated. The view of the terraced fields of the farm, it's guest house, the rows of Dahlia, gladiolas and pears trees are beautiful. Crossing this, the village starts. Some of the houses have been constructed on the road side. Co-operative stores and Govt. office have come up here in the process of development and modernization.

During 1966 to 1972 whenever we came to Sangti on foot, some times with my family, the gaonbura and other familiar faces used to meet us at the kakaling with chhang, Ara and salt tea. We used to sit together and discuss individual as well as social matters with frankness and open heart. Even the matter related to differences between the Couples which some time resulted in separation were also arbitrated by me. The people gave me unlimited affection and respect and I enjoyed the feeling of oneness with them. But again when I came to this very place during the period 1981-83. I found the whole environment changed. The same old familiar faces looked strained and aloof. The party feelings which started during the election of village panchayat and assembly divided the people and were present even after the elections. The system of sitting together of the villagers has taken atoll. I had to meet the different groups at separate places. But the matured and wise people of all these villages - Sangti, Khaso, Phudung, Khalibok expressed their sentiment and views that Monpa society as a whole is slow on the path of progress but very fast on the path of fashion. There is a tussle between the traditional leadership and the new elected leadership. Material success is eroding the spiritual value of the society. In the society where the difference between the poor and rich was non-existent, now has become very wide and distressing. The whole society is facing the trauma of fast changing circumstances. Nevertheless it is hoped that their deep faith in Budhism will hold them in their age old social, cultural and religious values even under these strong changing winds

The Monpas see nature in its intimate pitiless force and furry terrorizing the brave as well as timid and their child-like character impels them to worship the more proximate agents which seems to visibly wreck their crops, flocks, and vex them with disease and disaster. In July' 1967 I got an opportunity to witness the ritual worship of forest-God called Lhasoybin. These dieties are established as protector of Budhism and ritual scripts have been prepared for performing their worshiping. Lhasoybin is one of the ritual in this tradition.

The forest God is worshipped also in villages Rahung, Khoitam, Tawang and Miji area. In Miji area they sacrifice a mithun where as in Monpa areas animal sacrifice is prohibited. In Dirang village there is a stone platform where the villagers assemble and rituals starts at night. Each of the seven clans of Dirang village collectively called Chan-jum select a priest representing their clan. Phyichhun Pa clan being more in number select two priests. These eight priests are called Bonpu. The rituals are performed standing. No book is read. Every half an hour these Bonpu observe a break and consume chhang or Ara. The villagers attend the ritual after their evening meals and stay for the whole night. The Bonpu also sacrifice either a chicken or sheep or Goat as the Lamas do not perform animal sacrifice. The villagers return to their houses in the morning after completion of the ritual. Lhasoybin is also called Chhisoybin.

Similarly on the outbreak of any epidemic and eventuality of bad crop KANGSO ritual is performed. This is solemnized in the village gompa by the Lamas. To organize this, villagers appoint two or three executors who are called "chupon". They collect chang, Ara and other items used in the rituals from each house and bring it to the Gompa. During this ritual the entry inside the village or going out of the village, agricultural and other activities are totally prohibited. The Lama prepares six TORMA by kneading wheat or barley floor BongBokpai with Ara, Jaggery and red sandal powder. These Tormas are prepared a day earlier to kangso and kept at night on a wooden plank inside the Gompa. Yak butter lamps are lighted near them. It is believed that as these Tormas are offered to deities no rodent or animals can touch it. Next day from 4 O'clock in the morning to 6 o'clock evening the lamas performs the ritual by reading KANGSO-PECHA. In intervals after every chapter DANG, and

BUKCHI are played in fixed rhythm. The whole village maintains a peaceful silence. In the evening on completion of the ritual the Lama who is usually a family man joins the villagers in festivities of chhang, Ara and meals.

The Sherdukpens also observe such rituals called KHIKSA during the months of October and November which is performed by their village priest called JEJI. The auspicious date for this ritual is fixed by observing the closest approximate of the great bear to the moon. Each of the seven clans of Sherdukpen, Thungduk, Thungon, Thongchi, Khrime, Dingloy, Mosobi and Megezi select a JEJI to perform the ritual. No recitals from any book is done. The villagers collect food grains, PHA (CHHANG) and PHODKO (Ara) for this. In this ritual the Kachharis from foot hills of Assam also contribute paddy, Banana and Tambool wrapped in new GAMCHA. They bring these items up to Doimara from where the Sherdukpens carry these to RuPa. For this ritual a cock, a goat and a bull are selected by the JEJI. Once selected the owner hands over the bird or the animal happily without any cost. During the ritual the goat and the bull are kept garlanded and after the ritual set free to roam around. Every year these selected bird and animal is brought to the ritual. Only after their death new bird and animals are selected.

We had been celebrating in the traditional way the new year "LOSAR" in the month of February corresponding to their month of DAWA DANG PO. It is believed that during this month Budha obtained the inner enlightenment to achieve NIRVAN. The locals also believe that if there is snowfall during Losar the New Year will be more prosperous for them. The Monpas follow the Tibetan Lunar calendar. According to which the dates eighth, fifteenth and thirtieth are auspicious. Chaitra - Sankranti, Makar sankaranti and

Budha Purnima are considered very auspicious. On the fourth day of their sixth month they celebrate "Lhabab Duchen".

It is believed that on this date the Bodhisattva of infinite mercy Avalokiteshwar voluntarily descended on the earth even after attaining Nirvan to liberate all beings from their worldly fetters and sufferings. On the third day of Losar prayer flags are put on all Monpa houses. The roof are decorated with bunch of small prayer flags called "Fohing". For putting large flags the lama performs a rite called THRUI. He sits at the base of the prayer flag, chants a litany inviting the divinities to come and take their seat on a small metal mirror called Melong, set in a metal bowl and with a Khada placed on it. He pours water from Bumpa to bathe the divinities. Then he consecrates the prayer flag with Ramne in which he chants a religious formula and occasionally throws a few Namkaling and grains of barley and rice towards the prayer flag. Namkaling is seed of a plant with two white petals attached for facilitating wide dispersal. It is a substitute for flowers in Tibet and can be preserved for long period. He follows it up with another rite called sorkem. In this he puts some barley and rice in a metal cup placed on a bowl, Chants a litany and occasionally pours Ara over the barely and rice. The assembled villagers then shout in chorus Lha so Lo and Ayi-hu hu. They smear each others forehead and face with flour of barley. The Losar festival and feast continue for a fortnight. People take bath in the hot water spring down village Lish and wear new clothess.

During the Monpa month Dawa - shunPa carrosponding to the nonth of April, on the fifteenth day a fair is organized in village - Lagam Gompa. In the fair people come from all the villages of this area and also from Tawang and Bhutan. A colony of tents surround this small village - Lagam. Ponnies, mules, and crowd of villagers, abundance of chhang and Ara and the rising smoke from the fire-hearths made outside the tent, creates an unique scene. In the Gompa there is a stone with image of Budha, said to be imerging over the stone miraculously, is worshipped.

Namshu village celebrate the festival of "Gahden namchhut" in the month of November for a week from 23rd to 30th. In this there is no dancing and merrymaking for the first two days. It is said that during this period the originator of Gelugpa sect Chongkhapa left this world and went to heaven. This religious festival is also called" Eibdor" or 'AtaAibee" in vill-Namshu. After two days the elderly men and women perform mask-dance in the village Gompa courtyard and the dance competition, continue for the whole night.

People of the Ningma sect conduct the ritual called TSER JOMO during the month of July- August which corresponds with the sixth month of Monpa DawaDUKPA. The Lama recites THOKHAOR-ROLPA in the Gompa of Ningma sect or in one of the house of Ningma people. The recitals ends at mid night. After that all the male members assemble at some high spot over the village and descends on the village with burning torches and pass through the houses shouting. In the burning torch they throw the powder of pine tree resin to inflame it. The Torma made during the ritual is put in fire to drive out the satanic forces from the village. According to their belief Budha attained enlightenment on the fourth day of the sixth month. The religious families celebrates DUKPA- CHESIH and recite NAMGEMA.

The monpa lives in an atmosphere of the marvel. They are ever on the outlook for the omens and the everyday life is governed by superstitious regard of lucky and unlucky days. No story is too absurd for them to believe if only it be told by

Lamas. These have no relation with the Buddhist faith and probably originated long before its introduction. It had become an important part of this areas sub culture. These omens are to some extent similar to the beliefs of the people of certain areas of other States of India. Hair cutting and nail cutting in evening after sun set, sweeping the house floor and throwing the dirt out side at night, and blowing of the roof in bad weather are considered bad omen. Seeing a snake or python approaching in dream is indication of death. Meeting a young girl carrying vessel full of water, centipedes and bees dwellings in the house are good omen. On the birth of a child, the Lama consult the book KARCHI and predicts the auspicious and inauspicious dates. The Lama consults another book NAKCHHI on the death of a person to tell the date and time of taking the body out of the house and for last rites. All other activities like marriage, construction of a new house, repair of old house, making irrigation channels, castration of an animal commence only after consulting the book DRECHHI.

In Dirang village we got invited to a house warming function after construction of a new house. In the new house a Lama was reciting from the book "Lhapsang" near the altar. The altar was decked with yak butter lamps and offerings of Tsampa and currency notes. After the recital of Lhapsang, the Lama consecrated two prayer flags called Dumphan and gave to the house owner to put one in the front side of the roof and another on the back. Both these flag poles were then connected with a string and small flags were tied to the strings at intervals. After that the lama accompanied with a member of the new house who carried a Torma in his hand circumambulated the house three times. The Lama was leading and beating the Dang in hand, followed by a group of four-five naked men only in lion-cloth shouting and jumping.

The Torma was thrown outside the perimeter of the house. It was explained that in case while bringing timber and stones from the forest and mountains the Gods, demons, tantalus etc dwelling in the forest and mountains have been displeased, the offering of the Torma will pacify them and save the house from their wrath.

Prior to the construction of the house, the soil of two to three sites were taken and shown to the Lama. The Lama approved the soil of this site only as an auspicious site and fixed a date for laying the foundation. On that date the lama performed the ritual of earth breaking by reciting two books - Nangshar Nange and Tashi-pecha and sprinkling the ground with rice and wheat. The construction of the house commeced after this. From the three main beams of the roof, in the front as well as in the rear about two feet long wooden phallus were hanging. This is for warding of the evil eyes. According to the tradition these wooden phallus called Lakteng, should be brought to the place by the sister of the house owner on her back. Prior to tying them on the beam, these are consecrated by the lama and Khada is tied to it. After that the beams are hoisted on the roof. Such wooden phallus were seen hanging from the beam of every Monpa house.

Nine Km from Dirang is the village-Lish, whose dialect as well as the customs are to a large extent different than the Monpas of Dirang. The inhabitants of Lish are also Monpa. For anthropologists their dialect, customs and traditions could be a very interesting study. The monpas of this area neither can understand nor speak their dialect, but the people of Lish can easily understand and converse in the Monpa dialect. With the main village there are two separate hamlets called Lishgompache and Lishgompalog. People of these two hamlets speak the Monpa dialect. The prevailing belief is that the people of vill-Lish came from "Nakchhinmun" means a large dense black forest full of elephants to this place via Bhairavkund and Kalktang.

The older generation of Lish related their origin from Dergaon in Assam. From Dergaon they migrated to Amartala plains near Udalguri. This was an area of thick virgin forest referred by them as Nakteng Tankha. In due course they migrated via Kalaktang - Domkho - Morsing and came to the present place. It is estimated that this village was established near about the time when Lhageyala Gompa was constructed. The people of Lish, generally called Lish Pa were also collecting tax from the Kacharies of their old place in Assam. Later on this right was taken away by the villagers of Morsing and Domkha.

The LishPa who are followers of Ningma sect have also retained their old rituals of worshipping, which is different from the Monpas of this area. On the 27th day of the new year Losar they organize religious festival called Mangakurum in their village community hall called "chhobrang". Subscriptions in cash and kind are collected from all the houses including the two adjacent hamlets. The Lama recites Domang for two and half days. On the third day in afternoon the Tormas prepared during the rituals are kept outside on the three sides of the village on a wooden platform about nine feet high. The first Torma is kept fifty yards away from the kakaling constructed on the path coming from Rama Camp. The second and third are kept on the first and second Manc built on the track coming fron Dirang village. During the ritual coming inside the village or going out from the village is completely prohibited. To indicate this prohibition a five feet pole on which 108 twigs are tied on the upper end, is stuck in the ground on the paths coming to the village.During these three days everyone including the Lama enjoy the chhang unabashedly. Torma is prepared out of barley flour. Some are also made of clay. One particularly strange thing which came to the notice was the dress of two persons who were taking the Torma outside the village. One was dressed like a person from plains of Assam and the other like a Miji. For both of them speaking in Lish dialect was a taboo. They were to speak in Assamese and Miji dialect. They believe that even by mistake if they will utter a single word of their own dialect, the demons will over power them and cause grave harm to them. These two persons go to every house in the main village as well as in the adjacent hamlet and collect edibles, spices and cash. The edibles and spices are equally divided and kept with the Torma. Cash is distributed among these two persons and the interpreters who move with them. Some villagers narrated that when they were going out to the area of Bhairav Kund to collect tax, they had to return to the village prior to this ritual. Otherwise they could come to the village only after conclusion of this ritual. In this ritual no animal sacrifice is done.

Another such ritual called Torduk is observed in the eighth month Dawa Gupa corropsonding with June-July. This is also called Moriso Eshi. During this period the cattles are taken up on the high meadows. The Lama recites Domang for three days in Chhobrang. A pig and a sheep are killed by suffocating them. Both these sacrificial animals are kept in chhobrang facing the Torma. On second day a live fish is kept on burning pyre made of peach twigs. On the third day between three to four o'clock in the evening a group of young boys assemble above the village and with burning torches of dry bamboo descend to the village along with the lama shouting HO-HA and visit all the houses. The Lama carry a highly inflammable powder with him which he occasionally throw on the burning torches to produce bright flames. This powder is prepared from the rotten rhodondron tree trunk. The rotten tree trunk is pulverized in fine powder which is then fried in a pan. This is called Marja. During this ritual all the hearths are cleaned and the fire and ashes are thrown out side the village. On the third day they take the fire a fresh from chhobrang to lit their hearth. On the same day the Tormas numbering seven to eight are kept out side the village in the field towards Dirang village. The villagers make a bonfire in the field in which they sing the tip of their arrow and shoot upwards in the sky. The Tormas are then offered to the fire. During this ritual all agricultural activities are prohibited. As far as possible the people prefer to stay in the village.

For three days another interesting ritual is organized in the Chhobrang during their tenth month Dawa Chupa corresponding with the months November-December. This is called Jima Lama Wang and conducted by a tantrik Lama Duba. The Lama who lives in Jima Gompa in the jungle above village Nyukmadong has a different look. He had long beard, matted hair in a bun on the top in which a small silver Damru was tied. He was invited along with his assistants. He recited the scriptures brought with him for three days in the Chhobrang. These Lamas live near cremation spots or in isolated places in the forest and only after achieving some tantrik power, come to stay in a Gompa near the villages. For this ritual every house prepares five Bre flattened maize from the new harvest. Bre is the wooden measuring pot equivalent to approximately eight hundred grams. The gaonbura brings the wooden box in which the common property of the village called yanggam containing the last years Torma, antique silver coins, grains etc before the Lama. Jima Lama opens the box and the last years Torma is distributed among the villagers as Prasad. After the ritual new Tormas are kept inside this box along with grains and coins, locked and sealed by Jima Lama and given to Gaonbura for safe custody. On the second day Jima lama along with his assistant conduct the Hawan called lingse. In this the root of Dub grass, aromatic leaves from the plants found at high altitude, chakpa Sha, Namkaling, Ghee, Til, barley, wheat, paddy, Rice, Maize, Millet etc are offered in the fire.

The third day is observed as the day for blessings- wang. All male, female, children offer some cash and obtain wang from Jima Lama. The cash offering is usually a handsome amount which is taken by Jima Lama. It is believed that after this ritual they will have a good crop of buck-wheat and due to this ritual the frost will not harm their crop.

LishPa were averse to marriage relations outside their village. The people of Dirang and Sangti area also were not inclined to have marriage relations with Lish Pa. But this has been relaxed now. In vill Lish the prominent clans are Thankhar, Jamkhar and NeyermuPa. Besides them other clans are TatPachan, Usubichan, Wamulingchan and Ngajimbichan. Marriage within the clan is taboo. For all social and religious rituals the married Lamas are called. After three days of the birth of child Keskar Lama is invited for naming the child. On the event of death for performing the last rite chiskar Lama is invited who accompany the funeral procession up to the cremation spot called Dutho.

Towards East-North of vill Lish is another wide valley of Chug. Hamlets on both side of Chug Ri, and the crops in the fields are quite impressive. On the far end of the valley the green meadows, blue forest and mountain looks very majestic. In these forest wild animals like deer, sambhar, barking dear, Takin dear and leopards are found. Going ahead the village and fields one can see the ground ploughed by the wild boars.

In 1982 during the visit of DalaiLama, Arunachal Pradesh Government constructed a new Gompa for performing Kalchakra ritual. It is named Jangchhub Chhoyaling Gompa. The Dalai Lama also consecrated the nearby Gompa in S.S.B. Camp. During his fortnight stay in Dirang, the valley was crowded with people from Arunachal, Sikkim, Bhutan and Tibet.

This valley of Dirang and Sangti starting from Mandla - Phudung to Lubrang to south of BangaJhang and SELA is the most fertile, prosperous and developing place. Planting apple, peach and plum, which commenced in 1967 by the horticulture department is now thriving in this valley.

Monpa Woman

Azilhamu Dancer

Mask Dance

MonPa girls from Vill-Lish

Dirang Valley

Dalai Lama blessing the author with Khada

Gompa in SSB Camp at Dirang

CHAPTER THIRTEEN

Arts And Crafts of Monyul

The unique feature of tribal art is the presentation of natural untainted beauty. Their paintings, handicraft and arts are neither for self expression nor is art for art sake. Similar to the ancient Indian art which was primarily hieratic in character and ultimate aim was to depict deities and religious rites, the Monpas and Sherdukpens art is based on the tradition that making images of deities, religious symbols, and Lamas is a pious act leading to salvation. In its evolution and development, therefore the art is in the nature of Sadhna. Further since according to Budhism the self does not ultimately exist, self-expression is of no real value. Beauty has no meaning apart from divine life whose inherent quality is truth and goodness. The depiction of devine figures is considered a support to meditation and devotion. Except for Islam, all other great religions have believed in the visual representation of their religious ideal and this has inspired the creative impulse universally.

The paintings and handicrafts of Monyul have a distinct influence of artistic style from India, Nepal and Tibet. Buddhist art reached a high degree of excellence in India, the country of its origin and when Budhism came to Arunachal Pradesh via Nepal and Tibet it came as a doctrine belief and philosophy accompanied with highly developed art forms as visual aids in comprehension. The people of Monyul, showed their unique ability by using their indigenous mineral and vegetable paints which are highly suited to the style and purpose of their art and the climate.

The aim of art in Monyul is primarily to serve as visual aid for understanding the abstruse tenants of Buddhist philosophy and religion. One of its main subject is making Mandala or KHYILKHOR. Everyone cannot paint this. This requires special intense training and those who are able to attain proficiency in this art are called Khyilkhor-Lopon.

Mandala is basically a mystic complex geometrical pattern. In it within a circle, a number of triangles, rectangles, square, hexagon etc are imposed and painted in bright colour. The opening designs are different for each deity. The khyilkhor for ChenRejig, Sange, Chhana Dorjee, Jampeyang and Kalchakrayan are varying in design and colour.

Among the Khyilkhors, the most complex and remarkable is the mandala of sixteen Arhats with Budha in the centre and the four guardians in each of the four gateways. The philosophical explanation of Khyilkhor is very difficult. Mostly it is used for initiation and religious ceremonies. The accompanying rites are believed to be means by which microcosmic man can achieve harmony with the macrocosmic universe through visualization of the divine pattern.

Through the paths made in the pattern, the person in meditation enters in to the Mandala and comes out after that.

Khyilkhor are made at the auspicious hours of initiation and performing the religious rites. It is prepared with coloured powder or in fine coloured sand on a flat surface. The khyilkhor-Lopon uses thin hollow bamboo tubes full of different colour of powder or sand. He sits with full attention to his task holding the hallow bomboo tube in his right hand which rests on his left hand wrist. With slight vibration, to the tube he traces the outline of the khyilkhor, and completes his creation. On completion of the particular religious rites the khyilkhor is disassembled and immersed in some River. But some khiyilkhor are painted on wooden panels and fixed in the ceiling of Kakalings. Now khyiklhors printed in press are also available.

Another popular art is making of the eight auspicious symbols called "Tashi- Tagey" these are –

i. The banner of victory - Symbolizes the victory of enlightenment.

ii. The parasol of authority - Authority of Budhas teachings.

iii. The Conch shell - Reverberating sound of Dharma.

iv. Golden Fish - The eyes of gnosis as fish can see through muddy water.

v. The knot of eternity - Representing the theories and philosophy of rebirth and resurrection

vi. The wheel of religion - The eight spokes representing the eight paths-Astangik Marg.

vii. The vase of immortality - Immortality of the soul.

viii. The flower of compassion - The ultimate goal, Enlightment.

Or

The lotus flower

Above these signs three jewels representing Budh, Dharma and Sangha are traced in a bowl called NORBU.

These eight auspicious symbols are extensively used in Gompas, in the houses, on Almirahs, cupboards, walls, windows etc. These eight symbols are made separately and also in a combined design. These are painted in bright colours and also carved on wooden panels.

Another masterpiece of the Monyul painting is Tankha. Tankha is a painting made on white cloth or canvas of different deities and manifestations of lord Budha. A piece of especially treated white canvas is tightly fixed to a rectangular wooden frame to prevent any crease during painting. In proportion to the size of the cloth the outline sketch of the painting is traced. The sketching of different parts of the body like hand, feet, fingers, toes, eyes, ears, nose are also made in perfect proportion. Putting colour in the sketch comes after this. On completion, the painting is placed in an attractive frame of coloured brocade. The brocade strip at the bottom is wider than the strips put on the top and sides. On this broader strip in the centre a piece of different colour brocade is sewn. This is called the "door" to the Tankha.

The Tankha is not only the product of creative self expression or the desire to depict beauty. It is mainly the object of worship. In the centre of every Tankha there is the painting of a tutelary deity. To reach the deity there has to be a door. Thankha is also made of appliqué work on silk brocade depicting numerous subjects of tantrik Budhism. Among these the most popular are of lord Budha, Guru Padamsambhav, his two consorts and the eight emanations and also of Tara in white and green colours. In all these Tankhas the proportions of the figures of different deities, the folds in their dress, the Mudras are all depicted in strict accordance with the tradition. The colour schemes of most of these Tankhas are marvelous. Golden paint is prepared by mixing gold powder in a particular chemical. This paint is used specially in showing the details of the dress. This was strikingly visible in the age old Tankhas. In Jangchhub Chholing gompa of Dirang which is popularly known as Kalchakra Gompa, there is a twentyfour feet long Tankha depicting the mystic yab-yum made on silk and brocade appliqué work.

It is unfortunate that the greed of commercial art dealers have started using fabric paint in preparing the Tankhas. Such Tankhas are meant for decorating the wall of drawing room.

In the paintings, besides the eight auspicious symbols Tashi Tagey, seven precious objects are also depicted in breath taking colours and style,

i. AKHOR NANGYAL- victory wheel. This wheel is on the stupa at Sanchi.

ii. NORBU CHINDEN - Chintamani Ratna.

iii. LHENDUP CHUPDEN- Minister of supreme caliber.

iv. EIYOG CHHOKSI CHUNMO- The devoted female gem.

v. LANGPO CHHE the white elephant

vi. LUNGTAR SKEYPS- The winged horse

vii. PALDEN JOKHEYAM MAO - The brave commander in chief.

The tantrik monogram NAMCHU WANGDEN is another important subject of painting, wood carving, stone sculpture and engravings on silver lockets. This is found on the doors of the .houses, on the wall of MANE and silver lockets worn by the women folk. In this monogram the ten letters of Lhenja script are arranged aesthetically. The Lhenja script is of seventh century. Some book of this script is said to be with the Buddhist of Newar clan of Nepal. This script is called RanJan or RanJa in Nepal. Now this script has vanished.

On the walls and ceilings the paintings of different Gonpo and CHOSKYON who have found place as protector of Buddhist religion are depicted in multicolours.

The offerings of Pushpa, Deep, Gandh, Geet, Mala, Nritya and Lasya pleasing the divinity have been personified as fairies and painted on the walls and ceilings of the old Gompas. Although now faded due to many years of incense stick smoke, these paintings are still remarkable. These are shown in the painting like Pushpa (METO-MA) as a fairy in white with flower in her hands, Deep (Nangsal-MA) in red colour with a lamp in her hands, Gandh (Dri-Cha-Ma)in light green colour holding a conch shell with perfume, Geet (Lu-MA) in pink colour with veena in hands, MALA (Prenba -MA) in yellow colour holding a flower garland, Nritya(GAR-MA) dancing fairy in green colour, and Lasya (Gegmo-Ma) in a couquettiesh attitude holding a mirror In ivory complexion.

In the wall paintings, the depiction of VAJRA BHAIRAV God of death, Yamantak considered as prominent divine figure in Gelugpa, is very frightening. Amidst many heads of this divine figure, the head of a bull is painted below are seen, the many hands hold different type of weaponry and below the feet stampeding many figures of deities, tentalus, titans, humans, beasts and birds. Besides this in wall paintings a depiction of Devas (Lha), Nag (LU) Yaksha(Nobin), Gandharva (Drija), Asur (Lha MAYIN) Garur (Namkadin) Kinnar(Miamchi Indra(Gyabin) YAM (SINJE) Varun (Chu-Lha) Kuber (Nod Sbnim) Agni(Melha) Marut(Lung-Lha) and Brahma (Chhanspo) are seen.

The art of sculpturing clay statue have been achieved to the extent of perfection. In the Gompas many statues of different sizes- small and large are seen. In these the very common are the statue of Sange, Chhana Doorjee, Jampeyang and of Avalokiteshwar. The most popular statue of Avalkiteshwar is of four hands. Two hands are shown folded in prayer while the other two hands holding a lotus flower and rosary. In Dobley Gompa above Lumla the large clay statue of Avalokiteshwar Chenrejig is of thousand arms and eleven heads. The facial expression on all the eleven faces is the shining example of the expertise achieved by the sculpter in making this statue. Above the eleven heads there is a figure of YAN, another manifestation of Avalokitsshwar. On the face of YAN the depiction of fear is skillfully shown.

Among the clay sculptures, the most remarkable are the eight statue of Guru. Padamsambhav in Changprong, Sangeling and Taksang gompa. The statues are hollow inside. At the time of its establishment and consecration Mantras written on hand made paper and Bhojpatra are placed inside. This is called Jung. This consecration rite is symbolic of Pranpratishtha of the image.

The depiction of different ASAN and MUDRA in the clay statues are perfectly visible. Mainly five Asans are seen depicting five "BHAVA". The VAJRA PALAN BHAV is depicted in the well-known crossed legged Budha posture. The soles directed fully upwards. In the pose of deepest meditation in which both hands lie loosely in lap.

The NIYAM PALAN BHAVA, the sub-active pose in which the legs are unlocked. The left being quite under the right and soles invisible. The SATVA PALAN BHAVA is the Bodhisatva pose. This is the pose of first emergence from meditation. The legs are loose, unlocked and soles are scarcely seen.

The LALIT PALAN BHAVA, the enchanters pose is depicted after the manner of enchanter MANJUSHREE. Here the right leg hangs down with an inclination slightly inwards and left is loosely bent.

The MAITREYE BHAVA is skilfully made sedent with both legs pendent.

The statue of Budha in nine different MUDRAS are seen in different Gompas. The statue of AKSHOBHYA Budha in earth touching mudra, AMITABH Budha in meditative posture resting one hand over other with the palms upward, in UTTARA Bodhi Mudra index finger and Thumb of each hand are joined and held in contact with the breast at the level of the heart, DHARMA CHAKRA mudra In the dogmatic attitude with right index finger turning down fingers of Left hand. VARAD MUDRA, the bestowing mudra signifying charity in which the arm is fully extended and the hand is directed downward with outstretched palm to front. SHARAN MUDRA, the protecting mudra with arm bent and palm to front and pendent with fingers directed down wards. ABHAYA MUDRA with elevated slightly bent arm, palm to the front and fingers directed upwards. TRIKON MUDRA differs from Abhaya Mudra in having the thumb bent and when the thumb touches the ring finger it makes a triangle. This is the preaching mudra. The SAMMOHAN MUDRA pointing the index finger in hypnotic gesture.

The depiction of color and facial expressions in clay images is remarkable in the statues of twenty one manifestation of TARA. Among these prominently visible are the Green Tara (Dolma Nangmu) white Tara (Dolma Karmu) and Bhrikuti Tara (TO NYER-CHAN). This statue is dark indigo coloured and with three faces all frowning. Besides, these Prashur Tara supremely valiant, CHANDRA OJAS SITA TARA- White moon brightness Tara, GAURI TARA - The golden colour Tara, SARWA SIDHI TARA - The giver of prosperity, MARICHI - OJER CHANMA, the brightly glorious TARA and VAJRA VARAHI TARA the adamantine sow (DORJEE FAGMO).

The art of wood carving developed in Monyul. Wooden bowls made of tree galls are very common as it remains unaffected of heat of liquid. The door - frames, windows frames and the pillars with fine carving on them are seen in Monpa houses. On doors, windows and altars three carved wooden panels are arranged one over other in an aesthetic manner. These are called PEMA, PATA and SORSA. Besides these making low wooden tables called CHOKSI, the eight auspicious symbols TASHI TAGEY, the thunderbolt DORJE, dragon, and many more symbols are neatly carved on wood panels. For the dances different type of wooden-mask depicting human facial expressions as well as of animals are prepared. Some of these are painted in bright colours. Many of such masks in due course of time acquire a unique texture being exposed to smoke and dust.

In Tawang area people manufacture paper from inner bark of the shrub called SUKSO (The daphne cannabin). The paper is remarkably tough.

The architecture of monyul is seen in construction of the Gompa and Chorten. Chorten are similar to architectural style of STUPA with some changes. After death the human body dissolves in the five elements. The stupa is the replica indicating these five elements into which the body mingles. The solid base of the chorten indicates the Earth, the half round structure over it indicate water, the triangle on it fire, inverted vault of the sky AIR and ETHER by an acuminated circle tapering into space.

The art of Buddhist Monpas and Sherdukpen is completely related with the religion, whereas the arts and crafts of other tribes of Kameng – AKA, MIJI, BUGUN and BANGNI are more utilitarian and closer to nature. Their art in weaving, cane craft, bamboo-craft which include making needle to hair comb and the houses, tattoo - art. and other such skills are highly appreciable.

Weaving has been a basic necessity for MonPas, SherdukPen. Miji and Akaas. The Miji and Aka myth states that the humane body was in the beginning covered with hair and there was no need to cover them with cloth. Gradually, in course of time the humane lost these hairs and started covering them with bark of trees. Later on they learned to weave cloth. Weaving is mainly done by the women folk on waist-loom. This eighteen inches loom is fixed to the waist of the female and the other end to bamboo frame. The length of the threads five to six meters is wrapped around the wood or bamboo frame. The advantage of such small loom is that in inclement whether the loom can be shifted inside and in sunny weather the weaving can be carried out outdoor.

The weaving designs of MonPa, SherdukPen, Aka, and Miji are similar yet different in details for which they have different explanations. The Bangnee for their requirement of cloth visit the markets in plains of Assam. The Bangnees are skilled artisans in cane and bamboo work. They prepare thin threads out of cane and with these weave baskets, pouches, scabbard of Dao and furniture.

With the improved facilities of communication and advent of factory made items, the original art and craft have declined. In the effort of modernization and development the people are considering their art and craft inferior in comparison to the attractive goods from outside and have adopted cloths, plastic items, fancy imitation jewellery and cosmetics. With this trend, no wonder, when their original art and craft would be seen only in museums.

Eight auspicious symbols of Mahayan Buddhism

Namchhu wangden

CHAPTER FOURTEEN

Aka Area

South of Bomdila adjacent to Bugun and Miji areas is the 320 square K.M. area of Aka tribe. There are twenty one villages. The first encounter with the Aka was in village Jamiri in 1966 August when we walked from Jamiri Point to Jamiri village. Our programme was to reach Buragaon on the same day but the coincidental meeting with the Aka rani in village Jamiri and her requests made us stay for the night in Jamiri. She explained the woe of the village, the destruction of their maize crop by wild bears and asked us to shoot one or two bears that night. On this proposal of hunting bear, one of our group members Taibong got very enthusiastic and he recited many hazards of marching further in late afternoon to make us stay at Jamiri.

We got accommodated in the guest room called THUMONA of the house of Rani. The room remains vacant if there is no guest. We got the first impression of their good hospitality.

In the evening by 7 PM it was totally dark and we sat in the maize field on a bamboo platform (Chang) with the rifles and flash light. Within a few minutes we were attacked by black large mosquitoes and were about to abandon the hunt, when the bears entered the field and started plucking the maize cops. Two of them came near the chang at a distance of thirty feet. a shot was fired in the light of the flashlight and a bear was killed. The others ran away. Aka Rani and villagers expressed their gratitude and with the result we stayed in the village for the second day also.

There are twenty one villages of Aka tribe. In these prominent villages are Jamiri and Hussigaon and there is the position of one Rani in each of these two villages. The Rani is successor of Aka kings who ruled this area till late. Now the Rani helps the needy people, heads the village panchayat and act as counsel. In front of the Rani's house is the age old assembly place of panchayat called MELAYEE where many judicious decisions were taken. At this spot there is a platform and around it stone seats embedded is ground. This is a sacred place as their ancestors sat here and made important decisions. In other villages there is no such fixed place for MELAYEE. Usually the village panchayat is assembled in open. The village headman is called Gibba.

In Aka community along with king, queen and upper class there are slaves also. The slaves are called KHULO. These KHULO are from SULUNG tribe who are bought by Akas from their Bangnee masters. The KHULO community lives segregated and their children are also called KHULO. In the house of Rani such KHULOS are found working as domestic help. Their price is paid in kind like mithun, clothes and sometime in cash.

The second day a number of villagers came to meet us in the house of Rani. It was heavily raining. We were served with local beer LAUPANI and MINGRI along with rice and pork. After lunch, with the help of the interpreter we learned the local myths and got acquainted with the geography of the area.

According to one myth Aka, Miji and Bangnee had one common forefather Called BUSLO AOU. He possessed a magic herb called FA which was highly invigorating. He gave this herb to a large size rodent like animal called KHULJADUM. Their another ancestor SIBJAU ACHE snatched the herb from that animal and kept it with him. He gave this herb to his dogs and chicken as an experiment and it proved to be very invigorating tremendously improving the health of the animal and birds. This herb FA was later distributed among Aka, Miji and Bangni and is used in preparation of Laupani and Mingri.

At the house of Rani we were offered mingri in beautifully carved and decorated silver cups which are prepared by Miji craftsman. The Laupani and Mingri were brought in hallow bamboo containers called Schapsu. For storing water hollow bomboo pieces called SCHAOU and large bamboo water pipes called MON are used.

The residence of Rani was like other houses in the village constructed with timber and bamboo but larger in size and area. In the whole of Aka area only one design of the houses were found, constructed on five to six feet high timber and bamboo platform under which goats and pigs are kept. A single thick log on which wide notches are cut is used as stile to climb up. It required some practice to ascend and descend the stile. The front verandah is covered and adjacent to it there is the small room NEMKHWARI and after this the large family room ULURI. The ULURI serves as sitting, sleeping, cooking and eating room. In the centre of the ULURI is the fire hearth on which a three legged iron frame is kept. This is called ESCHEPRI. The fire in the hearth is kept burning constantly so that the ULURI is warm. At one side of ULURI is small store room RIN and on the other side a similar room to store fire wood called SEJAURIN. For storing grains a separate house called NECHI is constructed outside.

All the houses are constructed with the collective labour of the the villagers and no wage is charged or paid. On completion of the construction, the owner invites everyone for a feast and liberal offering of laupani and mingri. Now with the availability of cement and corrugated iron sheets, the houses are constructed using these materials and outside laborers are engaged.

The personality of Rani was impressive and dominating. The fifty years old Rani was adorned with silver ornaments which must have been weighing altogether about three to four kilograms. In the earlobe were large round silver ornaments called ROMBIN and GICHLI, in both wrists silver bracelets GEJJAIE, silver chain in neck called LHENCHI with a large round locket embedded with turquoise and coral called MELU. The other significant trait was the red glow spreading to the outer core of lips due to constant betel chewing and the blue tattoo line in the centre of forehead and down on the chin with two more lines making a triangle. Out of strong curiosity we wanted to know about the tattoo. It was explained in a normal tone by the Rani that she got this tattoo at the age of ten. All Aka girls of that age get this tattoo. The method of tattoo is very simple. The line is scratched on the skin with a long thorn of a particular bush and juice of another creeper is squeezed on the deep scratched line. This juice also works as antiseptic ointment and the lines get the blue colour. Along with tattoo there is the tradition of piercing the ear lobe in the childhood of the boys and girls both. A bamboo dart called FUSBA is put in the ear. Later on the silver REMBI is worn in the ear.

We prepared tea using our ration and offered it to the Rani. But in spite of our request she refused to take the tea. Our interpreter explained that in Aka community taking milk or any preparation made out of milk is taboo for the women folk. Even any thing cooked in the utensil which contained milk is taboo for them. If the women folk will drink milk or take any milk preparation, there will be large red eruptions on their skin. We were surprised to hear this. We further explained that the tea is having condensed Tin milk and may be accepted. But the Rani did not accept our tea. The only reason one can visualize is some incident of skin allergies after consuming milk or milk combined with some other food item must have afflicted the women folk of Aka, which made them believe that milk is harmful to the women folk.

The third day we departed for Buragaon thanking Rani for her hospitality. Aka called themselves HRUSSO. The name Aka is given by the people of Assam. The faired skin, light blue and brown coloured eyes HRUSSO used to visit plains of Assam with painted face for trade. The Assam people called them OKA MANU means people with painted face. The word OKA means painting or sketching. From OKA-MANU the word AKA came into popular use.

An old myth states that the capital of BANASUR was at the bank of Brahmaputra River at Sonitpur, the present TEZPUR. Banasur and his sons were killed in the battle by Krishna on the episode of Usha and Anirudha love affair. The grandson of Banasur, Bhaluk took shelter in the hills of Arunachal Pradesh with the remaining kins men and women. The Akas are the descendents of Bhaluk and Bhalukpong was their old place.

According to Dr. varrier Ellwin, the ancestors of Akas, were driven away by Krishna and Balram from ParatpGarh on the bank of River Giladhari, which is north of present Biswanath Charali. Both these narrations indicates that Akas are from Mahabharat period.

The Akas collect tax called POSA from the villages situated in the foothills of Assam. After the Ahom kings, the Britishers also recognized their right to collect POSA. According to C.H. Heiselmeyer's book Indias Nort-East Frontier in Nineteenth century, in the year 1825 the Akas used to collect from every house a bundle of cotton thread, a garment for their female, a Gamacha. The Akas were having their own king. The story of TAGI RAJA is still popular who in the year 1835 attacked and destroyed the military post of Britishers at Balipara. A truce was signed between Akas and Britishers in the year 1844. But in the year 1888 the Britishers had to send an army detachment in this area to rescue some officers who had gone to Aka area and were kept there as hostage.

These officers had gone there to collect some agriculture tools, samples of their handicrafts and cloth for an exhibition at Calcutta. They had also asked some men to accompany them in their full tribal gear and ornaments to Calcutta. This was wrongly interpreted that these officers had come to take the king and queen with all their ornaments to Calcutta. This wrong interpretation and publicity hurt the sentiment of Akas and they detained those officers. In 1914 captain Neville visited this area with an army detachment and established friendly relations with the Aka.

Buragaon is one of the prominent village of this area and also the administrative headquarter. The view of sun set from this village was unforgettable as the hill ridges all along change colour from green to blue to dark.

There was unusual gaiety in the villages one evening. On meeting the Gaonbura, we were invited to this festivity. A match maker from vill Karangania had come with proposal from groom side to the house of the bride in Buragaon.

Such match-makers are called MUKHAOU. After many rounds of the Mukhaou, the bride family had accepted the proposal and the village priest called MUGGAOU had sacrificed a chicken and observing the liver of the chicken, declared this relation auspicious and acceptable. The festivity was the reception of Mukhaou and Muggaou.

In Aka society marriages are negotiated and fixed on acceptance by both the sides. Some incident of elopement also take place when the boy and girl are smitten with love. Marriages between Aka and Miji are also solemnized. But marriage in the same Gotra (clan) is not permitted. In Buragaon only there are five different clans who called themselves -DUSUSO, KHABITISO, JEBISO, SICHISO and PALAJIN. These clans are also in village Jamiri and HUSSIGAON. In karangania there are four different clans - SAGRASAMA, KERLUSAMA, TIPESA and TIRIN. Besides them CHIDISO, FOMIJISO, PARIYIJISO and GALASO are in village - Dijungania, CHIDISO and WECHSO in vill - YAYUNG, JESUSO, SASUSO, RUGJUSO, FUSISO Clans are in vill - SAKRIN and PALATHARI clan in vill PALATHARI and PALIJI. Marriage outside the clan is recognized and the role of MUKHAOU is important in this, but if the MUGGAOU declares the proposal inauspicious, marriage won't be solemnized. MUKHAOU gets handsome reward from the groom family for his many rounds made to the village of the bride, for his tact and skillful talk in getting the proposal accepted.

In the rites of marriage, important one is tying by the priest on the right wrist of the bride, the family ornament ESCHERI presented from groom side with a thick thread of sheep wool called FOKKI. Even in incident of elopement and love marriages, the marriage is solemnized by tying ESCHERI and FOKKI. In marriages the bride-price once agreed is immediately paid. If the bride-price could not be paid due to some financial strain, it could be paid in installment. The disputes in marital relations arise only when bride price agreed to is not paid. Besides this re-marriage of a widow is also recognized. Younger brother can marry the window of his elder brother but not vice-versa. One can also marry the younger sister of his wife. Polygamy is prevalent. But incest is not at all tolerated in the society. Inter clan marriage is prohibited but marriage between maternal uncle (MAMA) and niece (Bhagini) is permitted. Some time, if the groom is unable to pay the agreed bride-price but still is eager to marry, the price is paid with his labour by staying in his would be in-laws house. During this period often physical relation between the boy and girl is established and child is born. If necessary, they have to stay in separate house but in all eventualities the fixed duration of his service should be completed by the boy in bride- price. Usually two to three mithun, one Eschepri and five to six pairs of clothes are given. The small piece of cloth is called EMISA and the larger one OSCHA GAMOSO. Besides this the groom side has to give a pair of clothes to the brother of the bride. It is called SADAR. Collectively this offering of clothes is called BASA.

After a few rounds of Laupani and Mingri the group of young boys and girls rose up for their traditional dance BRAJAVA. One young man took the percussion instrumental SETI and other the cymbal called THAMULU. On the rhythm of the percussion instrument and cymbal the taping of feets started with the word Adi -YE-DA-DIDA. First the line of girls stepped forward moving their both palms and wrist in a delicate coquettish manner and slowly moved aside. After this the line of young men on the rhythm of Adi-YE-DA-DIDA came forward and danced with fast tapping of their feet exhibiting the youthful vigor and enthusiasm. The movement of their wrist and swaying of waist was also faster. The dance continued for quite some time with pause for Laupani and Mingri. The VRAJAVA dance changed into another style of dance called CHHAKKAUDO and SADI NUKCHHO in which there was no song they danced on the rhythm of SETI and THAMULU. There was no indication of these dances coming to an end, even after late night. We quietly left for our camp, seeing the host unaware of our departure. We had to cover a long distance next morning.

We left Buragaon early morning and reached village karangania by 10AM. We halted in the staging hut of the village and planned to leave for vill- Dijunggania after lunch. While the Lunch was being cooked, we got the glimpse of the red-coat of the GaonBura who had come to meet us. With the customary compliments of JAIHIND we asked the Gaonbura to take a seat and offered him some tobacco leaves which are very much liked by them. We found the Gaonbura worried. He was telling something in his own dialect to one of our AKA Jawan and seemed to have not getting a satisfactory reply. On enquiry we came to know that his wife is having pain and swelling in one of her feet and he needs medication for her. We took our medic bag and left for his house. Climbing the high platform of his house over the single log with notches for foot rest used as ladder we came to the rear veranda of the house called Nemkhwari. On examination of the sole of the feet it was found that a thorn had gone inside and now the whole area is full of puss. With a slight incision the thorn and puss came out. We applied ointment and bandaged the wound. We came to ULURI, the large living room where the Gaon Bura with some villagers was awaiting us with LauPani. We accepted it honoring the sentiment of Gaounbura. With the round of Laupani and help of our interpreter we came to know that to recover from this ailment they have to worship a certain deity. In fact the worship of deity THAMU can save them from blood related ailments. The disease of heart and intestine is caused due to displeasure of deity CHOLEMUS and Gynecological diseases due to displeasure of deity NAMS. The pleasures of deity HUMISISE-JUMIRIRI bestow riches and prosperity.

The religious concept of Aka's are directly related with the pleasure and displeasure of natural forces. According to their belief the destiny of man is controlled by the natural forces. On their this belief, they have the four prominent Gods- SKY, Mountain, Earth, and River. Besides these four there are other deities. Among the deities also most important is TYARO, The beneficent one, whose blessing bestow happiness. The worshiping ritual of TYARO is conducted during the mont of April when the fields for Jhoom cultivation is ready. The duration of this ritual festival varies from two to ten days on the selection and availability of Pigs, chicken and Mithun for sacrifice by the village priest MUGGAU. During this period all activities like collecting firewood from the forest; hunting and agricultural works are suspended. Entering inside and going outside the village is prohibited.

For the wellbeing of cattle wealth, once in three years the ritual sacrifice of a mithun to deity JINHE PINTE MURJE is carried out. Sudden death, accidents and sudden illness are attributed to the anger of deity PAMLEGRI. To please him sacrificing a cow is a must. Just before sowing seeds in the field. the MUGGAU performs the sacrifice of a pig or chicken to the deity BI-OYESCHE for good harvest. The deity BI-OYESCHE protects their crops till harvesting from wild animals, diseases and natural calamities. After such ritual no female who is in her menstrual period can go near or pass through the fields. It's believed that the seeds will rot and harvest will be very poor if such female go near the field. For happiness in family, good health of female members, begetting children, safe delivery of children, the deity BRANGO and his consort SIKCHI-ESINSA are worshipped. The ritual with sacrifice of a sow or hen is conducted for two to three days and all activities during the period remains suspended.

They also believe in ghosts, black magic and miracles. The ghosts and ethereal powers are called CHIGJE. But practicing black magic is considered evil and social offence. On detection of this practice the village panchyat takes severe view and imposes heavy fine on such person. In such type of activities, frequently used is the magic of hypnotizing called SURRAU, to which the disappointed young lovers take recourse to. The most complicated and difficult ritual is SUTOUN-SOBJIYE in which head of a cow, or bull or a mithun as well as sacrifice of the wild animal PHULATMO JOU are required. The ritual to harm ones enemy "PHUKHU SISTO CHASRA" is conducted with the help of the tooth of tiger or leopard, wild boar, bear, and snake. Similarly in performing another such black - magic SIJAU, - sacrificing a dog and sprinkling its- blood is done. All these acts are performed at secret isolated places, therefore witnesing such act was not possible.

Next day we left for village - Dijunggenia and after three hours walk reached there. This is one of the largest village of Akas. Unlike Jamiri, Buragaon and Karanggania where houses are spread over, here the dwellings are made adjacent to each other. On arrival we were greeted with BA KHINA YA means how do you do. We also replied NO UDA - we are well. And shook hands. At the edge of the village was the staging hut where we spent the night.

Ahead of Dijunggania, for reaching vill - PICHANG one has to descend to River kyari on which there was a single cane rope tied to bamboo anchors at each side. In this single Strand of cane were two round cane loops. For crossing the River one has to climb the bamboo platform to reach the loops, lie down face upward between the loops, placing one under the arms and putting the legs into other and propel himself with his hand on the single cane rope to reach on the bamboo platform at the other end. After crossing the River the climb to village- Pichang starts. The villagers of Dijunggenia and Pichang both come to the River for fishing. Next day we also went to the River for fishing and having the feel of the bridge. In the evening while coming up to village our attention was drawn to a melodious song MUKHSHA MEMSA LAMASU CHHE. This is a popular love song of Aka, sung by the young boys and girls in solitude, expressing their longing to meet each other.

Aka Couple

CHAPTER FIFTEEN

Miji Area

The Miji area is adjacent to Monpa and Aka areas. The administrative centre of this area is at NAFRA. The main habitat is in the Valley of Bichom River and its tributaries DIKRI and DIYANG. The villages of this tribe is up to LADA-BESAI in East Kamang. According to the census of 1981 the total population was 2602 only but their area is larger than the area of Aka tribe.

In 1967 we had visited the villages and area from NAFRA to MATHAU and BULU at both sides of DIKRI River via villages DICHIK and DIBBIN. We started on a trekking along River Bichom up to AZANG PHU the source of the River. On first attempt we could go up to village. NAKHU (1575 mtr.) Heavy continuous rain for three days compelled us to take shelter in the house of the gaonbura Sri Dongcha. It was not possible to venture outside the house due to very heavy rains. We could communicate with the gaonbura in a language using Hindi, Assamese and a few words of Miji-dialect. To pass time the rounds of drinking chhang in silver cups continued. In intervals the group of small children came and sat surrounding us. We entertained them showing pictures in the magazines and books brought with us. After three days when the rains ceased, the gaonbura advised us not to proceed ahead. The temporary wooden bridges on many streams between NAKHU and JANG had been washed away. We returned to Dirang via Nafra.

Next time in June '70 we took up this expedition. This time we had a number of Miji Jawans of this area as guide. After Nafra we stayed for a night at Nakhu. This was a five hours march. Leaving Nakhu in the morning, we reached HamnaJang (1800 mtr.) by noon and after taking lunch there reached VETONG by evening. Up to this destination the track was not bad and we could cover a long distance. The track passed through snake infested area but we did not came across any. Vetong is the last hamlet of four houses in Bichom valley. A little distance from vetong to east is another hamlet DEBRI, also called DEVAI. We spent the night in the house of the village SARDAR. He painted a discouraging picture of the terrain and track ahead but we were determined to go ahead. We started early morning and reached to the bank of River DIYANG by noon, negotiating narrow tracks over steep rocks. Over the River was a single cane Strand with two cane rings. We crossed the River one by one by hanging in the cane rings and propelling ourselves with our hands. By evening we reached VAMTHUNG. This was an old camping site of Assam rifle. There was a large plain ground inside the thick forest, a clear water source and enough dry fire wood. We made our bivouc with groundsheets on rocks. The fear of snake was haunting us as this terrain was snake infested. Early morning we made a reconnaissance of the area. Near by we found a grassy plain ground measuring 150'X100'. This served as drop zone for air supply to the Assam Rifles contingent. Fourth day we reached GOLAI (3520 mtr.) after ten hours march. The track was obliterated due to overgrowth of vegetation. Golai is also camping site for Assam rifles contingent. Old Jericanes, tin boxes and other left over scattered in this area marked it as a camp site. We spent the night at Golai. From here we could detect signs of two tracks. One going towards west-north across Bichom River to BOMPI and other straight north to HABANG (3660 mtr.) through Azanghpu. Our mission was to visit the origin of river Bichom, so we left Golai next morning and reached Habang by ten o'clock via Azangphu. The weather was favorable but due to high altitude the severity of cold increased. A light drizzle started and due to fog the visibility was poor. Between Golai and Azanghpu we saw large flock of colourful Pheasants. Patches of snow were at many places. At Azangphu five small streams coming out of the snowy range meet together and make a large stream which turns into River Bichom. The ground all around was marshy and it was very damp and cold there. We crossed Bichom at Azangphu and reached Habang. Scattered, left over items and marking of a volleyball court gave an indication of camp site. Also nearby was a plain ground measuring three hundred by two hundred feet which served as a drop zone for air supply. The bad weather made us leave Habang and we returned to Golai via Azangphu. On Sixth day of our expedition we came back to VamThung via wabrang. It took six hours while coming back as the track was descending. On seventh day we were at Vetong. From vetong a track goes to Poto following the western bank of River Bichom. It is two days march towards north and another two days towards west to reach Poto. This track is frequented by the hunters only as the whole area is rich in wild animals. From vetong we did not go to Najang but came to Mathau via Delong and Dichhin. Villages. We crossed River DIKRI between Dichhin and Mathau. After crossing River Dikri the track to Mathau was a stiff climb and very tiring. We had left Dirang ten days back and now decided to complete the expedition in short stages. After only four hours march from Mathau we reached Dibbin and halted.

From Dibbin we came to Nafra, from Nafra to But and reached Dirang after a fortnight.

In this expedition in our group were Monpas, Sherdukpens, Bangnee and Miji Jawans. At village Nakhu while communicating with the Gaonbura Dongcha we came to know that the Miji call the Tawang monpa BAMI and Dirang Monpa Netchang.

The Monpa in their own dialect call the Miji, GIDU. But the Miji prefers to call themselves Dammai.

Later on, I visited NAFRA and khelong on several occasions. There are many similarity between Miji and Aka. In Miji community also marriages are ex-clan. In Khelong there are three main clans - Thri, Lekang and Jajang. Other clans are - Deruj, Sudanjo, Ningsengsomo, Throngjangsomo and Deru.

Polygamy is prevalent. A man can have up to seven wives. All the wives live together under the same roof. But there is no polyandry. Joint family system exists. If there are five brothers, all of them after their marriage will stay in the same house with their separate hearths. The oldest or the youngest of them will look after their parents. The houses are built on a platform normally five feet high from the ground on strong timber poles having a dimension of fifty to sixty feet in length and twenty feet in width.

The Miji are hospitable community and in their houses there is a separate room for the guests. Earthen pots and hollow bamboo pieces as containers are used in the houses. A few aluminum and brass utensils, procured from Assam are in use. Miji do not make earthen ware. These are procured from But Monpas of vill -Jirigaon. In prospers Miji houses we saw silver ornaments, cups, tobacco pipes and scabbard of Dao.

Artisans expert in silver -smithy and silver filigree works are in Miji villages. The dress is similar to Akas and they don a cap like Akas which they call SHAPOJANG. Their domestic drink is fermented Laopani (CHHANG). They do not distill and prepare strong alcoholic drink. Chhang stored for a number of days acquire a stronger bitter taste and becomes more intoxicating. It is called Mingri. The area has abundance of cane and bamboo and the houses are constructed with these. Another item in abundance is Rangbang (NUMANK) flour made out of the dried pith of palm like tree. Rangbang is also used in preparing Chhang.

Slave system was in this community. In villages, families of Sulung tribes are kept as permanent servants. The village panchayat Ammai and the village headman Nokhu wield great influence. NOKHU means the senior old man.

Nafra to Buragaon in Aka area, there is a well beaten path via MIRIKA and BICHOM and this distance of thirty seven Kms is covered in one day. Buragaon to Thrizino also the distance is almost same and the track goes via salji, karangania and kararamu. In our next expedition we went to Seppa in east Kameng from Nafra. From Nafra it took only two hours to reach kelong-Khajalang. From kelong a track goes down to village NIJONG and other towards right to vill - Lapusa. From Khajalong the path is a steep climb. After covering some distance there is a stream and from the right side of the stream there is another track, on which after six hours march is vill- Chalang. Chalang is a Miji village of eighteen houses. The climb from Khajalang is so steep and tiring that one has to spend the night midway in the jungle before reaching the next stage Janasing. From Janasing the vill-chalang is at a distance of three hours march. Vil! - Chalang is in two parts. Upper part has only six houses whereas the lower part has twelve houses. From Janasing we reached Bameng via Sikang. Jarkam, Apong, upper Liyak and Saitok. Jarkam and saitok are sulung villages.

Slung are considered primitive tribe. They depend upon Miji and Bangnees for their all needs and are treated as slaves by them. The main habitat of Sulungs is in Pachuk River valley. Their villages are Bombayee, Hapobe, Paksa, Jarkam, Nishang Jang. Pio and Satuk. Other sulung villages are Rava, Pardung Sulung, walong, sario, saria, and Donkhong. During the decade sixty and seventy when some sulung young boys were recruited in S.S.B., their Bangnee masters lodged strong protests and did not allow them to return to their duty place when they went on leave to their villages. However, in the 1980s, some sulung young boys were recruited once more. The administration also initiated measures to free them from slavery and provide education, agricultural implements, and seeds for agriculture. Some programmes for their social, economic, and intellectual upliftment were introduced. The sulungs now go by the surname PRUIT.

Another large Miji habitation is in LADA-BESAI area. This area was first visited by us in 1970. In 1983 again we visited the area with Miji and sulung Jawans from Bameng via Pachuk River valley making short stay in sulung villages. The pronunciations and style of speaking the Miji dialect is completely different here from the dialect spoken in Nafra area. Lada is a group of small hamlets. These hamlets are Nuvlong, Salong, Vabenglong, GraikJang, vakke, Drakshi and Sekhang. Our main stay was in vill-Drakshi. The people are very hospitable. By evening the group of young boys and girls used to assemble at our camp with their local instruments - changlong hadol and Nin for singing and dancing. After an early dinner of rice and meat, accompanied with chhang and

Mingri, their group performed the dance Namsung which started with the song:

Nakho Busoto Namrue songre
Dine Noi stui changro songre
Nabuiju stui weken songre
Narmaiju kiyu dakan songre.

Namsung is specially performed on the occasion of construction of new house. But these carefree young boys and girls perform this dance as and when they desire to do so. The usual dance and song for the evening entertainment is:

Neyebuju Rieo Nemeju Rieo
Chodong poinase, Re Re yu o Nase
Nakho buraieo, Nakho Noraieo
Bukha chho nase, ndang me nase

Chhijo buraieo, chijo naraieo
Logese nirase Longho Nirase
Pancha Sojaraieo me bhavo jurieo
Sulai nirase mailai nirase
Babu ji Raieo Saheb Jurieo
Dhanji Sahab Nase guto renase.

They keep on dancing on this song which means

O young boys and girls.
Beat the drum and cymbals
Let us dance together
O friends and girls
This is the time for merrymaking
O panchayat members
This is not the time for hearing complaints

O Babu and officials
This is not the time for office work.

In Miji community the village panchyat in Nafra area is called Ammai whereas in Lada area it is Sojung. The village priest is called Thromi and kevaie. They worship their God Sujang Noi for getting children. To get protection from all ailments and trouble they, worship Sunjang Jomyonoiying. This ritual is conducted by the Kevaie in the house for ten to thirty days. On the fixed auspicious day a Mithun, four to five pigs and more than two dozen chickens are sacrificed. The Kevaie himself does not eat the meat of the sacrificed animals, but the front right leg and thigh of the mithun, pig, and a chicken are given to his family. Besides these, a live mithun is offered to Kevaie. It is believed that this ritual will free and protect the village from all evil powers and bestow peace and prosperity on all of them. They also believe in sorcery but refrain from causing harm to anyone.

In marriages the role of the middle man is important. To initiate a marriage proposal the groom party sends a pig to the family of bride. Once the proposal is accepted the bride price called Nuikai Mall is negotiated and agreed. The marriage date is fixed by the Bangro. Bangro takes the bride and the bride party to the house of groom and performs the marriage rites. Love marriages are also common. The influence of modern education, cinema. Video, television is propelling speedily the society towards fashion.

Miji girl

Miji Woman

CHAPTER SIXTEEN

Bangnee Area

East of Bomdila beyond Aka and Miji areas, the land is inhabited by Bangnees of Kameng division. Even before formation of administrative districts of East Kameng, the administrative centre of this area was at SEPLA. There was no road up to Sepla till 1972. In 1966 we had reached SEPLA on foot in six days from Jamiri point covering a distance of 143 kms via Buragaon, Karangenia, Dijungania, Pichang, Sila and Phinche. Over the River Kameng was a steel wire rope bridge to reach the administrative centre at SEPLA. The S.S.B. camp was set up at the eastern end of the valley adjacent to the landing strip by the side of a stream after clearing the overgrowth and cane forest. The then Adl: Deputy Commissioner Sri K.D. Menon extended all help in establishing the camp. In his office, we got an opportunity to go through the dairies of previous Asst. Political officers which gave us an insight in the history, geography and social custom of this area.

After staying for ten days at SEPLA we moved for BAMENG. Another administrative centre. After marching for about ten kms we reached village Talong and got a taste of Bangnee furor. That day a religious ritual was going on in the village and movement in and out of the village was strictly prohibited. We had violated this custom. We were surrounded by a group of villagers in no time who expressed their anger shouting in their dialect making furious gestures and declared a fine of Rs. 500.

This made us nonplussed. But Lance Naik TAIBONG of our party came forward unslinging his rifle and started talking in the same dialect with the same furiosity simultaneously moving the bolt of his riffle backward and forward. This counter offensive was unexpected and so forceful that the villagers stood awe struck. Over and above this the acting by Galong. Miniyoung and Bokar Jawans making all sorts of gestures by taking out their Dao made a tremendous effect on the villagers. The whole drama ended in ten minutes, and the tense atmosphere amazingly changed into a pleasant one. The villagers welcomed us, stating that this is their own force. They mistook us for outsiders at first sight because of our khaki uniform. They were looking at me suspiciously and asked a few questions, which were answered by Taibong, and this satisfied them. We were made to stay in a large bamboo house. Within no time, the gaonbura came with ten villagers, and we sat together. They had brought APONG the local bear in hollow bamboo containers and we offered them cigarettes, match boxes and tobacco leaves. Our medic attended to a few sick persons in the village and gave them medicines. We spent the night peacefully in Talong.

We left next day for Bameng, the administrative centre situated at an altitude of approximately 5000 ft. By the sunset we climbed up to Bameng and the first sight which attracted my attention was a well-tended rose garden of about twenty-five different varieties of roses in full bloom in front of a dilapidated basha. On entering the garden, a dark, lean, thin short man welcomed me and shaking hands said "I am Dr, Paul." We came to know that Dr Paul was the most popular person in that area not only as a proficient physician but also a compassionate human being. Dr. Paul pursued his hobby of rose gardening, and had tremendous self-confidence. The other interesting character I met was the administrative officer Mr. S.T. Lha. Next morning I was invited for the breakfast. At the breakfast I found Mr. S.T. Lha and Dr. Paul slightly embarrassed. The reason was that there was no air-drop of wheat flour by Kalinga Airways and in the breakfast Halwa was prepared out of the flour of Rangbang which is the flour of the dried pith of a palm like tree. It was pink Jelly like but tasty.

We left Bameng for Chyang Tajo, another administrative centre via Khenewa. At ChyangTajo we stayed in the camp of 21st BN of U.P. P.A.C and next few days visited the villages Langpho Tajo, Namchar Bagang, Doripo, and Laching Bagang meeting the villagers and establishing friendship. After a week we returned to Seppa via Pipu.

The Bangnees were hitherto addressed as Dafla. In late 1966 they started objecting to the word Dafla and calling themselves Bangnee. They believe that their ancestors came to this area from Sarli-koloriyang region of Subansiri via Nyopin crossing the high ridge via Lolam Ragam pass and settled in eastern Kameng About Lolam Ragam, they could only state that it was covered with snow. Their lion-cloth Gingtam Aging and their style of tying the hair in a knot on the front of the head called Damatam Padam are adopted from the Tagins.

The name Sepla was also changed to SEPPA which means plain land or wet cultivation area.

After this maiden tour of the area we took another route via Lamdung, Takochili and Siejusa to reach Tezpur covering a distance of 110 kms. The track was infested with leeches, mosquitoes and snakes. While returning a large group of villagers accompanied us, who were coming to Itakhola market for their items of daily need. The four days agonizing foot march was turned into fun due to their company. They laughed and made fun of us whenever anyone of our group slipped and fell on the muddy leech infested path. But they also extended all help in covering the distance and we became good friends.

In 1970 and again in 1982 and 1988, I got several occasions to visit east Kamang and spent few days in the villages with old friends. Their houses are similar to the houses of Akas and Miji made of bamboos. The nomenclature of different part of their house is in their own dialect.

Polygamy is practiced in Bangnee community and well to do parsons take usually three to four wives. They pay Mithun, pigs, cows, Eri cloths, Dao and APONG as bride price to the family of the girl. The women folk are very fond of silver ornaments. They wear silver ornament Rungkhiyong in ears, bracelets in hand called KonJi and a number of beads garland in neck called Tasang. In their ankles they wear four inches wide anklet called Lakheng woven out of thin string of cane.

One can make out seeing the tightly fitted Lakheng, the skill and labour used with patience in weaving it.

The atmosphere of the village changes in the evening with shout of Aoul, Aoul, which is used to call back the Mithuns from the Jungle and Goye, Goye to summon the pigs. The fire in the mekrang is made to rise in flame and the living room NIYANSO is filled with smoke for some time. The main dish consist of rice, meat, bamboo shoots. The local drink is APONG fermented out of maze or rice. Apong is taken by all male, female and children. The evening meal used to be over early, and the villagers used to come and sit with us for gossiping. They used to clap their hands and dance to the beat of the drum. Females did not participate in dances until 1970. Only the male used to dance on the most popular song.

Odang Dangne Padam Dangne.
Olo Rine Bolo Rine
Take Sounje Korin.
Sabin Konjo Aou Jogchi
Sain Konjo Sali Char Chang.
Odang Dangne Padam Dangne.

The Bangnee celebrate the festival Moyokam from 24th to 27th February every year at central places like Seppa, Bameng and ChyangTajo in which a Mithun is sacrificed. They also worship evil power called Aiyu. The rites are conducted by their priest called NEBU or DODDAI. For this ritual there is no fixed place.

The bangnee male are by nature proud and carefree. This is reflected in their song

O! Nawanga hanme ne navatalo kavDono
Gondi Talo Do!

O! Gondi esi emang rele nakam satamko
Dosa tongsa konPo rene Kano rene Do!

O! Gondi esi emang rele nakam satam Ko
Gidam sera konpo rene kyang kyong aduk !

In bangnee community tender aged girls are married to aged persons. Those who can afford to pay good bride - money, marry younger girls. The girls could not oppose this openly but they express their anguish in songs. The tune of these songs are very touching. One such song frequently heard is -

Chauko minglena daugun minglena.

Anyo no nongme pupa peno

Halok miyungpa mo re

Nyobe nyose Koching moda

Anyo no nongme pupa peno.

Similarly after marriage the separation of the girl from her parents are expressed in songs. The songs starts with the lamenting melody of

O PAPA, O MAMA :

Anyola, Abola!

Sabyo jonme yourming sonming

Anyola, Abola!

Hame nyanglongmeng sibobi,

Anyola, Abola!

Mapopinkpu Donamala Kojing Anya Koklonem

Anyola, Abola!

Nyongru Loktum sine Anya neno abo honyo ade.

The sentiment of an orphan girl in expressed in the song:-

Mo sila Laping tegpe barmai eke Ko
Ngo mi Silo haping anyo Hi peko mo.
Ngo silo haping tegle abyo Peko mo.
Ngo dekte nyokomo haping abi peko mo.
Ngo haping nyaphmai puko mo
Nak sideku bobi deko aji peko mo
Ngo silo haping tegle
Ngo mangru loktum dekung
Anya monkbung Deku.

During my last visit to Seppa in the year 1982, I was shown an overhanging rock with fossil of one large and two small snakes six kms short of Bana and forty five minutes' walk towards south from the road in the forest. There was a waterfall adjacent to this rock. There was a plan to devlop this area.

Counting 1 To 20

	Dirang Monpa	Tawang Monpa	Sherdukpen	Aka	Miji	Miji (Lada Area)	Bugun	Bangnee	Sulung
1	Thur	Thi	Han	Aa	Ngang	Kyo	Ja	Aking	Que
2	Nithing	Nyi	Ni	Khanji	Gani	Krang	Noey	Ani	Ning
3	Sam	Sum	Am	Ju	Gathun	Katam	Yin	Am	Om
4	Jwi	Bili	Jwi	Fi	Bili	Palyi	Bi	Api	Vei
5	Nga	Lhenge	Kho	Fum	Bungo	Pagang	Khuwa	Angu	Vo
6	Thung	Gro	Chuv	Je	Riyan	Rap	Rap	Akhe	Rak
7	Jum	Nis	Sis	Mra	Niya	Mya	Miliya	Kanu	Liai
8	Yo	Geyet	Sanja	Shi Khaju	Siki	Shukayi	Mihiya	Pini	Liyao
9	Ngu	Dugu	Dikhi	Shi Thu	Sithun	Stan	Deke	Kayo	Dang
10	Se	Chi	San	Hun	Lun	Lang	Sung	Cham	Showen
11	Sam Thur	Chi Thi	Sahan	Wala	Lunang	Polang	Sunaj	Chamla Aking	
12	Sam Niching	Ching Nyi	Sani	Ve Kwij	Lun Gani		Suna Negey	Chamla Ani	
13	Sam Sum	Chik Sum	Sa Um	Ve Ju	Lun Gathun		Suna Chim	Chamla Am	
14	Sam Jwi	Chi Bili	Sa Jwi	Ve Thufi	Lun Bili		Suna Bi	Chamla Api	
15	Sam Nga	Chi Lhenge	Sa Khu	Ve Thufam	Lun Bungo		Suna Khuwa	Chamla Angu	
16	Sam Thung	Chi Gro	Sa Chuv	Ve Thuji	Lun Riyan		Suna Rap	Chamla Akhe	
17	Sam Jum	Chi Nis	Sa Si	Ve Thumra	Lun Miya		Suna Miliya	Chamla Kanu	
18	Sam Yen	Chi Geyet	Sa Sanja	Ve Thurikhwij	Lun Siki		Suna Mile	Chamla Pini	
19	Sam Thun	Chi Dugu	Sa Dikhi	Ve Thusiu	Lun Sithun		Suna Deke	Chamla Kayo	
20	Khap Thur	Khayali	Kha Han	Wansa	Gani Lun		Akhyak	Chamini	